KV-676-294

CONTENTS

SYMBOLS KEY

The following is a key to the symbols used throughout this book:

✈ airport	▥ restaurant	▣ café
↘ tip	▪ shopping	◉ fine dining

t telephone   **f** fax   **e** email   **w** website address

a address   **🕐** opening times   **!** important

$ budget price $$ mid-range price $$$ most expensive

★ specialist interest   ★★ see if passing   ★★★ top attraction

HOTSPOTS
ORLANDO

Written by Lindsay and Pete Bennett, updated by Nick Selby
Front cover photography: Epcot® Spaceship Earth attraction © Disney

Original design concept by Studio 183 Limited
Series design by the Bridgewater Book Company
Cover design/artwork by Lee Biggadike, Studio 183 Limited

Produced by the Bridgewater Book Company
The Old Candlemakers, West Street, Lewes, East Sussex BN7 2NZ, United Kingdom
www.bridgewaterbooks.co.uk
Project Editor: Emily Casey Bailey
Project Designer: Lisa McCormick

Published by Thomas Cook Publishing
A division of Thomas Cook Tour Operations Limited
PO Box 227, Unit 18, Coningsby Road, Peterborough PE3 8SB, United Kingdom
email: books@thomascook.com
www.thomascookpublishing.com
+ 44 (0) 1733 416477

ISBN-13: 978-1-84157-568-1
ISBN-10: 1-84157-568-2

First edition © 2006 Thomas Cook Publishing
Text © 2006 Thomas Cook Publishing
Maps © 2006 Thomas Cook Publishing
Project Editor: Diane Ashmore
Production/DTP Editor: Steven Collins

Printed and bound in Spain by Graficas Cems, Navarra, Spain

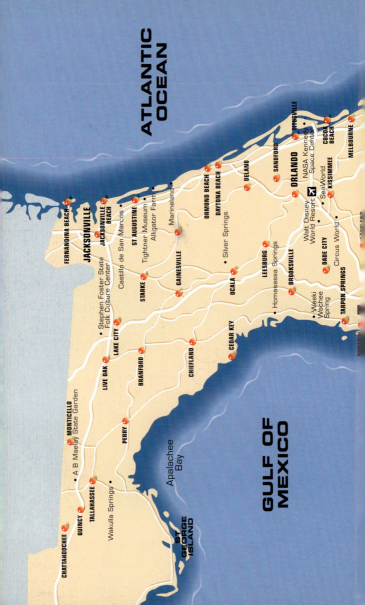

Getting to know Orlando

WHERE IS IT?

Orlando sits at the centre of Florida, the United States of America's southernmost state. Florida is a narrow finger of land on America's east coast, extending southeast, towards the Caribbean Sea; Key West, Florida's southernmost city, sits just 144 km (90 miles) north of Havana, Cuba. Orlando is only 75 km (47 miles) away from the east coast, 160 km (100 miles) from the west coast. Florida is a very flat state, with the highest point only 23 m (75 ft) above sea level.

THEME PARKS

Without Walt Disney, there would be no Orlando as we know it today. He bought up acres of swampland in order to create his **Magic Kingdom Park**. When visitor numbers exploded, other parks followed, and now Orlando is the best place in the world to let your imagination run riot. With the help of 100 cartoon characters, the best ride designers in the world and film gurus like Steven Spielberg lending a hand, it is easy to see why everything is so expertly done.

Today there are seven major parks, where you can spend at least one whole day each, not to mention a host of minor attractions that would be major pulls in other holiday resorts. Of its kind, this is top-notch entertainment not found anywhere else in the world!

SHOPPING

Orlando has become a shopping mecca for British tourists because the brand names are international, the quality of goods is high, and prices are at least 30 per cent cheaper than at home.

CLIMATE

With a temperature that rarely drops below 22–24°C (the low 70s°F) in the daytime, Orlando is a place where you can forget England's cold, grey winter days. Even Orlando's rain is warm. Summer temperatures average 35°C (the 90s°F), though summer days can be dotted by rainshowers.

◆ *Welcome to Orlando, in the heart of Florida*

The best of Orlando

Cruise on Daytona Beach (page 90)

Cruising in your car along the beach – what every generation of American teenagers dreams of doing in their first cars.

Discovery Cove (page 77)

The only place in Orlando where you can swim with the dolphins!

Disney's Animal Kingdom Theme Park (page 48)

The exotic animals from around the world at Disney's Animal Kingdom Theme Park make it Central Florida's most exciting safari park.

Disney-MGM Studios (page 51)

Watch a film being made, learn how Disney create their famous cartoons or take the plunge on **The Twilight Zone Tower of Terror** ride.

Epcot (page 44)

For the technology of tomorrow today, head to Epcot. Or take a global tour of the countries represented at **World Showcase**.

Gatorland (page 28)

Florida alligators of every size and lots of them!

Islands of Adventure (page 65)

Meet the cast of Marvel Comics and Nickelodeon and enter the world of Dr Seuss, not to mention amazing rides such as the **Incredible Hulk Coaster** and **Jurassic Park River Adventure**.

Magic Kingdom Park (page 40)

Orlando's original fantasy theme park, where it seems like a host of Disney cartoon characters have invited you to their personal, non-stop party.

NASA Kennedy Space Center (page 92)

Meet a real astronaut and touch a space shuttle.

SeaWorld (page 73)

The place to feed the dolphins and the stingrays, watch the gentle manatees at play, or get soaked by Shamu the killer whale.

Universal Studios Florida (page 60)

Universal Films and Hanna-Barbera get together to bring you movie magic, cartoon japes and some of the best film-themed rides in Orlando: **Twister**, **Men in Black – Alien Attack**, **Jaws** and **Back to the Future**.

Lake
Apopka

ORLANDO

HARRY P LEU
FORMAL GARDENS

Downtown
Orlando

EXIT
31

UNIVERSAL
ORLANDO RESORT

EXIT
259

EXIT
29

BEELINE EXPRESSWAY

ORLANDO
INTERNATIONAL
AIRPORT

SEAWORLD

DISCOVERY COVE

LAKE BUENA
VISTA

WALT DISNEY
WORLD RESORT

EXIT
27

EXIT
22

EXIT
10

EXIT
11

EXIT
14

CENTRAL FLORIDA GREENEWAY

EXIT
17

EXIT
26

EXIT
6

FLORIDA'S TURNPIKE

OSCEOLA PARKWAY

EXIT
3

EXIT
249

EXIT
25

MAINGATE

CELEBRATION

KISSIMMEE

EXIT
244

East Lake
Tohopekaliga

EXIT
24

EXIT
242

St Cloud

N

GREEN
MEADOWS
FARM

Lake
Tohopekaliga

FLORIDA'S TURNPIKE

0   5   10 km

0   6 miles

International Drive
convenient location

The original resort centre of Orlando, International Drive, known to everyone as I-Drive, is still the fastest growing tourist venue in the city. It has hundreds of restaurants, a choice of hotels for every budget, great shopping, and a range of inexpensive things to do, which means that you don't have to head to the major theme parks to fill your day. This is the best place to stay in Orlando if you do not want to hire a car. I-Drive is within easy reach of all the major parks by taxi, and some hotels provide courtesy transfer buses.

THINGS TO SEE & DO
Congo River Adventure Golf ★
Congo River now has two I-Drive locations to choose from and goes one better than its many competitors by offering prizes for great rounds. Plus, there are live alligators (small ones) you can feed. ⓐ 6312 International Drive (ⓣ 407 352 0042) and 5901 International Drive (ⓣ 407 248 9181) ⓦ www.congoriver.com ❶ Admission charge

Harry P Leu Formal Gardens ★ ★ ★
Take a break from the frenetic pace of tearing through Orlando with a visit to the serene former estate of business tycoon Harry Leu. The Leus were horticulture buffs who travelled the world, taking snippings back from around the globe to replant in their garden. The result is America's largest camellia collection outside California, a palm and bamboo garden, and Florida's largest formal rose garden. ⓐ 1920 N. Forest Ave, Orlando ⓣ 407 246 2620 ⓛ Open daily 09.00–17.00 except Christmas

Helicopter tours ★
Air tours around Orlando, starting with a mini-tour along the southerly section of I-Drive. You can take trips over some of the theme parks, especially thrilling at dusk when the nightly firework displays are underway. The ultimate tour takes you along the same flight path that the space

 *Watch out for the alligators at Congo River Golf*

shuttle uses when it lands at Cape Canaveral Air Force Base.

Air Florida Helicopters ❸ 8990 International Drive ❶ 407 354 1400
🕐 Open Sun–Thurs 10.00–18.00, Fri–Sat 10.00–19.00

Magical Midway ★

This is the nearest thing to a fairground complex on I-Drive. Magical Midway features an unusual elevated go-cart track, along with bumper cars and bumper boats with water pistols to wet your fellow riders and even passers-by on the street. Refreshments are also available in the complex. ⓐ 7001 International Drive ⓣ 407 370 5353 ⓛ Open daily, but times vary according to season

Orlando Science Center ★★

If you're travelling with kids, a visit to this world-class science museum should not be missed; films in the Planetarium are a treat, and the exhibits first rate. ⓐ 777 East Princeton Street ⓣ 407 514 2000 ⓦ www.osc.org ⓛ Open Mon–Thurs 09.00–17.00, Fri–Sat 09.00–21.00, Sun noon–17.00 ⓘ Admission charge

The Peabody Ducks ★

Ducks are mascots at the Peabody Hotel and a small group are kept in five-star luxury in a special duck-friendly room on an upper floor. Every day at 11.00 the ducks are escorted down to the lobby by a liveried chaperone, to swim in the fountain of the hotel lobby. They make their way back into the lift at 17.00. ⓐ The Peabody Hotel, 9801 International Drive ⓣ 407 352 4000 ⓦ www.peabodyorlando.com

Pirate's Cove Adventure Golf ★

A tropical pirate's hideout is the theme for these two mini-golf courses. ⓐ 8501 International Drive ⓣ 407 352 7378 ⓛ Open daily 09.00–23.30 ⓘ Admission charge

Ripley's Believe It or Not! Odditorium ★★

Robert Ripley is famed in America as an explorer and collector of strange and wonderful things. His museums are filled with the kind of exhibits that make kids squeal and squirm and where parents are bombarded with questions they cannot answer. Here, you will find a two-thirds scale model 1907 Rolls Royce made out of matchsticks and a grain of rice decorated with a beautifully painted sunset. ⓐ 8201 International Drive ⓣ 407 363 4418 ⓛ Open daily 09.00–01.00 ⓘ Admission charge

N

0 — 1 — 2 km
0 — 1 mile

DR PHILLIPS ROAD

TURKEY LAKE ROAD

UNIVERSAL ORLANDO
RESORT

ORLANDO
SCIENCE
CENTER

PRIME OUTLETS
ORLANDO

HOLLYWOOD BOULEVARD

PRIME
OUTLETS
ORLANDO

CINEMARK
FESTIVAL BAY

BASS PRO
SHOPS

SKYVENTURE   SKULL KINGDOM

INTERNATIONAL DRIVE

WET 'N
WILD

CONGO RIVER ADVENTURE GOLF

MAGICAL MIDWAY

UNIVERSAL BOULEVARD

KIRKMAN ROAD

PIRATE'S
DINNER
ADVENTURE

SLEUTH'S MERRY
MYSTERY DINNER SHOWS

7   **5**

EXIT
29

SAND LAKE ROAD

Little
Sand Lake

RIPLEY'S BELIEVE IT OR NOT! ODDITORIUM

HOWL AT THE MOON

TITANIC SHIP OF DREAMS – THE EXHIBITION

PIRATE'S COVE ADVENTURE GOLF

Big
Sand Lake

TURKEY LAKE ROAD

8   **2**

MASTERS OF MAGIC

1

HELICOPTER
TOURS

WONDERWORKS

6 **3**

9

4   PEABODY HOTEL

POINTE ORLANDO

EXIT
28

BEE LINE EXPRESSWAY

WESTWOOD BOULEVARD

SEA HARBOUR DRIVE

SEAWORLD

CENTRAL FLORIDA PARKWAY

EXIT
27A

DISCOVERY COVE

Skull Kingdom ★★

You have to walk through the gaping mouth of a skull to get to the ticket office of this medieval-style castle attraction. Once inside you will journey through ghoulish corridors, rooms and mazes with robotic monsters, a blood-curdling scary soundtrack and a few real-life shocks around every corner. This is a really effective development of the old haunted house attraction. 🅐 5933 American Way (at intersection with International Drive) 🅣 407 354 1564 🅦 www.skullkingdom.com 🅛 Open daily 11.00–22.00 🅘 Admission charge

SkyVenture ★

Want to feel the sensation of skydiving without having to jump out of the aeroplane? Soar on a cushion of moving air without a parachute and feel the sensation of free-fall without being more than a few feet off the floor. Training in the correct free-fall body position is given. Not suitable for children under eight. 🅐 6805 Visitors Circle (opposite Wet 'n Wild) International Drive 🅣 407 903 1150 🅦 www.skyventureorlando.com 🅛 Open Mon–Fri 14.00–midnight, Sat–Sun noon–midnight 🅘 Admission charge, reservations recommended

Titanic Ship of Dreams – The Exhibition ★★

Plunge into the world of the *Titanic* on its final voyage. This claims to be the first interactive attraction in the world and features genuine artefacts from the vessel itself. Recreations of the ship's interior make you feel that you are there and actors play the parts of passengers on that long, final night. You will really begin to understand the terror and despair that all those on board must have felt. 🅐 8445 International Drive 🅣 407 248 1166 🅦 www.titanicshipofdreams.com 🅛 Open daily 10.30–19.00 🅘 Admission charge

Wet 'n Wild ★★★

Orlando's original water park, Wet 'n Wild stays ahead of the rest with enough to keep the family occupied all day. The water chutes and wave pools remain eternally popular, as is the **Disco H2O**, an enclosed slide with a disco soundtrack, and the **Bubba Tub** – bobbing along in a giant inner tube. **The Black Hole** calls for a little more courage as riders are carried along a long, dark, twisting, water-filled tunnel, with the ultimate test of vertical body-slides 23 m (75 ft) high. 6200 International Drive ☎ 800 992 9453 (freephone in US) Ⓦ www.wetnwild.com ◷ Open daily, but times vary according to season ❶ Admission charge

---

Women should consider wearing a one-piece swimming costume here – the water rides can dislodge even the best-fitting bikinis!

WonderWorks ★★

You can't miss the WonderWorks building as you travel down I-Drive. The whole facade is upside down and the story is that this building has been ripped up by a hurricane and landed on its roof, complete with sections of pavement and palm trees! Once inside, WonderWorks offers a collection of over 80 high-tech interactive exhibits that will surprise

● *WonderWorks: how did that happen?*

and enthrall all ages. These include 'swimming with sharks' and what it feels like to be in an earthquake. The top floor is one vast arena where you can play laser tag (separate ticket). ⓐ 9067 International Drive, Pointe Orlando Mall ⓣ 407 351 8800 ⓦ www.wonderworksonline.com ⓛ Open daily 09.00–midnight ⓘ Admission charge

 If you can't walk far, **Walker Medical and Mobility Products** will rent you an electronic scooter. ⓣ 888 726 6837 (freephone in US)

EVENING ENTERTAINMENT
Cinemark Festival Bay ★
At the top of I-Drive near Prime Outlets Orlando, this cinema has 20 screens, which should mean you can find something to fill the odd wet evening that descends on the city. ⓣ 407 351 3117 ⓦ www.cinemark.com ⓛ Open daily 10.00–22.00

Howl at the Moon ★★
A cheesy romp of a duelling piano bar, in new digs. ⓐ 8815 International Drive ⓣ 407 354 5999 ⓦ www.howlatthemoon.com ⓘ Admission charge

Makahiki Luau at SeaWorld ★★★
SeaWorld stays open until late in summer and the shows always finish with a spectacular firework display. Perhaps the most spectacular show is the Aloha Polynesian Luau, with live music, dancing and tropical dinner. ⓣ 407 351 3600 ⓛ Open daily at 18.30 in summer ⓘ Admission charge (tickets sold separately from the general SeaWorld admission)

Masters of Magic ★★
A 90-minute high-energy Las Vegas-style show with grand illusions and tricks by Typhoon Lou and his team. Pizza and pop galore are available 45 mins before show starts, or you can opt for the show only. ⓐ 8511 International Drive (near the Ponte Orlando mall)

ⓘ 407 352 3456 🕐 Shows Wed–Sun at 18.30 and 21.00
❗ Reservations recommended

Pirate's Dinner Adventure ★★★

Swashbuckling galore at one of the most child interactive of the several dinner shows on offer. You are seated for dinner in a Spanish galleon and before long you are cheering for your hero and booing the rest. After the performance, stick around for the Buccaneer's Bash with disco music and fun dances. A five-course meal (including pre-show appetizers), as well as complimentary beer and wine, are included in the price. 📍 6400 Carrier Drive (off International Drive behind Wet 'n Wild) ⓘ 407 248 0590 or 800 866 2469 (freephone in US) Ⓦ www.piratesdinneradventure.com 🕐 Open daily from 18.30 (show starts at 20.00) ❗ Admission charge

Pointe Orlando ★★

There is live music most nights at the upper level of this shopping mall, where most of the restaurants are situated. **XS**, within the mall, has over 100 interactive games and simulators, and it is also a popular nightclub. The **Muvico Cinema complex** has 21 screens. 📍 9101 International Drive ⓘ 407 248 2838 Ⓦ www.pointeorlandofl.com 🕐 Open Mon–Sat 10.00–22.00, Sun 11.00–21.00 ❗ Admission charge to clubs

Sleuth's Merry Mystery Dinner Shows ★★

Think Cluedo on stage and you have the essence of this entertaining dinner show. If you solve the murder you win a prize. Three theatres and several different murder plots keep the acting fresh. 📍 8267 Universal Blvd ⓘ 407 363 1985 or 800 393 1985 (freephone in the US) Ⓦ www.sleuths.com 🕐 Open nightly 19.30 ❗ Admission charge

RESTAURANTS & BARS (see map on page 15)

🍴 **Bahama Breeze** $$ ❶ One of the few places on I-Drive where you can eat outside on their deck. Snacks include Mexican, Cuban and Thai dishes and the full menu features meat and seafood options. Live reggae and Caribbean music nightly. 📍 8849 International Drive

☎ 407 248 2499 🕒 Open daily 16.00 – 01.00 ❶ You must be over 21 to be on the deck after 21.00 or be accompanied by an adult

Boston Lobster Feast $$ ❷ Just as the name suggests, it is seafood and lobster all the way here, including an all-inclusive price seafood buffet that seems more popular than the à la carte menu. ⓐ 8731 International Drive (four blocks north of the Convention Center) ☎ 407 248 8606 🕒 Open daily 17.00–22.00

Dan Marino's Town Tavern $$ ❸ A great sports bar and restaurant owned by footballing legend Dan Marino. Drop in for a drink and bar snack or full meal. Menu includes steaks, chicken dishes, burgers and salads. ⓐ At Pointe Orlando, 9101 International Drive ☎ 407 363 1013 ⓦ www.danmarinostowntavern.com 🕒 Open daily 11.00–23.00

Dux $$$ ❹ Push the boat out at the elegant, up-market Dux, which offers a range of gourmet dishes, excellent wine list and impeccable service. ⓐ Peabody Hotel ☎ 407 352 4000 🕒 Open Mon–Sat 18.00–23.00 ❶ Reservations recommended; jackets required; no smoking

Olive Garden $$ ❺ This popular Italian family restaurant chain has a faithful following for its fresh salads, great pasta and pizzas. ⓐ 7653 International Drive ☎ 407 351 1082 🕒 Open daily 11.00–22.30

Race Rock Restaurant $ ❻ Spot the racing cars outside this ultramodern place, where you can eat surrounded by memorabilia and fantastic rock music. Menu includes snacks and full meals from burgers and sandwiches to steaks. ⓐ 8986 International Drive ☎ 407 248 9876 🕒 Open daily 11.30–23.00

Ronnie's Steak House $$$ ❼ A refined steak house with fine cigars and a reasonable wine list. ⓐ 7500 International Drive (free shuttle bus in I-Drive area) ☎ 407 313 3000 🕒 Open daily 16.00–22.00, happy hour 17.00–20.00 ❶ Reservations recommended

⬢ *Shopping on I-Drive*

🍴 **Sizzlers** $ ❽ An exceptionally good value eatery where you order and pay at reception, before heading to your seat to wait for your food. The buffet items are excellent, steaks done the way you ask for them and all the entrées are cooked fresh. Good food without the frills. ⓐ 9142 International Drive ❶ 407 351 5369 ⏱ Open daily 07.00–23.00

🍴 **Thai Thani** $$ ❾ This is a very good Thai restaurant with a lovely atmosphere and friendly service. The menu includes soups, curries, and even a full sushi bar. ⓐ 1025 International Drive ❶ 407 239 9333 ⏱ Open 11.00–22.00

SHOPPING

 I-Drive offers some of the best bargain tourist shopping in Orlando. You will find plenty of lower-priced souvenirs on sale, including many with a Disney theme – but watch the quality, as this varies greatly.

Bass Pro Shops: Outdoor World The place to come for your outdoor and tropical clothing, fishing gear and camping supplies. Very reasonable prices. 🅰 5156 International Drive 🅣 407 563 5200 🅦 www.basspro.com 🅛 Open Mon–Sat 09.00–21.00, Sun 11.00–16.00

Orlando Premium Outlet An excellent mall, technically in Lake Buena Vista, but the outlet is just off I-Drive (south of the main tourist area) and linked to it by an I-RIDE route. Prices for designer line ends and slight seconds are up to 40 per cent lower than the US high street – offering Brits an even greater saving. 🅐 8200 Vineland Ave 🅣 407 238 7787 🅛 Open daily 10.00–22.00

Pointe Orlando The newest shopping and entertainment area on I-Drive with stores such as Banana Republic, Abercrombie & Fitch, and other high street names. 🅐 9101 International Drive 🅣 407 248 2838 🅛 Open Mon–Sat 10.00–22.00, Sun 11.00–21.00

Prime Outlets Orlando Comprises what is also often referred to as the Belz Outlet Malls – more than 170 high-street-style shops which offer significant savings on overstocked items from retailers including Gap, Levi's, Eddie Bauer and scores more. Locals drive from miles around – it's not just tourists. There are two campuses. 🅐 5401 W Oak Ridge Road 🅐 4949 International Drive (at the northern end) 🅣 407 352 9611 🅛 All stores open Mon–Sat 10.00–21.00, Sun 10.00–18.00

Lake Buena Vista
popular and convenient

Walt Disney wanted to keep as much hotel business for himself as he could, within Disney's gates. The lower prices of hotels at nearby Lake Buena Vista cemented the city's popularity. That's still true, and while there's not much else here, with a rental car you quickly get to the parks or Orlando for an evening on the town.

THINGS TO SEE & DO
Pirate's Cove Adventure Golf ★
Pit your wits against 36-hole courses, through caves, over footbridges and under waterfalls. ❸ Crossroads Mall ❶ 407 827 1242 ❷ Open daily 09.00–11.30 ❶ Admission charge

RESTAURANTS
Bahama Breeze $–$$ This Caribbean-style bar/restaurant has an open terrace. You can dine or have drinks and listen to live reggae music. Great atmosphere after dark. Age restriction on the terrace after 21.00. ❸ 8735 Vineland Ave ❶ 407 938 9010 ❷ Open daily 16.00–01.00

California Grill $$–$$$ High-end Californian and American cuisine with light seafood and vegetarian specialities and a great view of the Disney nightly fireworks. ❸ 4600 North World Drive ❶ 407 939 3463 ❷ Open daily 17.30–23.00

The Crab House $$–$$$ The menu leans heavily towards seafood, particularly the Maine lobster and excellent crabs, but non-fish lovers can also choose from a range of chicken, steak and pasta. ❸ 8496 Palm Parkway ❶ 407 239 1888 ❷ Open daily 11.30–22.30

Hooters $–$$ A great range of dishes from chicken wings and onion rings to burgers, fish sandwiches and salads all served in informal fashion by the Hooters girls in their skimpy uniforms (be warned if you're bringing the kids!). ⓐ 8510 Palm Parkway ☎ 407 239 0900 🕓 Open daily 11.00–midnight

🍴 **Tony Roma's** $$ A great place for slightly smarter family dining, Tony Roma's concentrates on ribs (served with their signature BBQ sauce) but also serves a range of dishes including steak, chicken and seafood platters. ⓐ 12167 South Apopka-Vineland Rd ☎ 407 239 8040 🕓 Open Sun–Thurs 11.00–23.00, Fri–Sat 11.00–midnight

SHOPPING

Lake Buena Vista has a number of small open-air malls, including **Palm Parkway**, **Shoppes at Vista Centre** and **Crossroads of Lake Buena Vista**. These shopping centres have a range of shops, but by no means the selection available on I-Drive, although Crossroads (☎ 407 827 7300 🕓 Open Mon–Sun 10.00–22.00) is convenient to Downtown Disney Marketplace, where there is a good choice of genuine Disney souvenirs.

Bargain World and **Athlete's Foot** Two large bargain sports stores. ⓐ On the main State Rd 535, also called Vineland/Apopka Rd, which cuts through the resort 🕓 Open Mon–Sat 10.00–21.00, Sun 10.00–18.00

Orlando Premium Outlet Hugo Boss, Giorgio Armani, Tommy Hilfiger and Calvin Klein at discount prices (see page 23). ⓐ 8200 Vineland Rd ☎ 407 238 7787

Lake Buena Vista also has one large outlet mall, **Lake Buena Vista Factory Stores**, with a range of designer names at outlet prices. ⓐ 15591 S Apopka-Vineland Rd (on the east side of I-4) ☎ 407 238 9301 ⓦ www.lbvfs.com 🕓 Open Mon–Sat 10.00–21.00, Sun 10.00–18.00

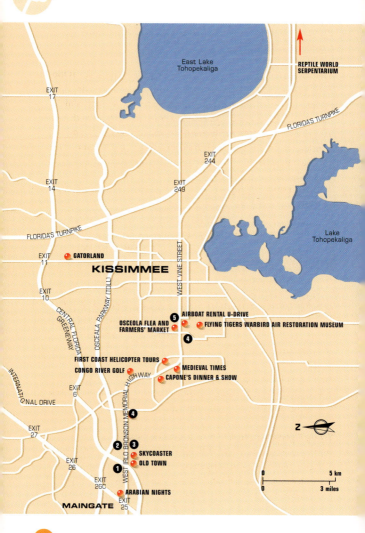

East Lake
Tohopekaliga

REPTILE WORLD
SERPENTARIUM

FLORIDA'S TURNPIKE

EXIT
17

EXIT
244

EXIT
249

EXIT
14

Lake
Tohopekaliga

FLORIDA'S TURNPIKE

EXIT
11   GATORLAND

KISSIMMEE

EXIT
10

⑤ AIRBOAT RENTAL U-DRIVE

OSCEOLA FLEA AND
FARMERS' MARKET   FLYING TIGERS WARBIRD AIR RESTORATION MUSEUM

④

FIRST COAST HELICOPTER TOURS
CONGO RIVER GOLF   MEDIEVAL TIMES
                        CAPONE'S DINNER & SHOW

④

INTERNATIONAL DRIVE

EXIT
6

EXIT
27

② ③ SKYCOASTER
         OLD TOWN

①

EXIT
26

EXIT
260

ARABIAN NIGHTS

MAINGATE   EXIT
25

CENTRAL FLORIDA GREENEWAY

OSCEOLA PARKWAY (TOLL)

WEST VINE STREET

WEST IRLO BRONSON MEMORIAL HIGHWAY

0 ___ 5 km
0 ___ 3 miles

Kissimmee
miles of attractions

The city of Kissimmee's main drag, Highway 192 (also known as Irlo Bronson Memorial Highway and Vine Street on various sections), comprises over 9.5 km (6 miles) of cheap hotels, restaurants and attractions. Highway 192 is so long that it's essential you check where your hotel is in relation to the main attractions. Some hotels offer transfers to the Disney/Universal theme parks, but it is best to have your own transport.

THINGS TO SEE & DO
Airboat Rental U-Drive ★★
You can pilot your own airboat along the narrow creeks that cut through the tranquil and unspoilt wilderness around Kissimmee. **ⓐ** 4266 West Vine Street **ⓣ** 407 847 3672 **ⓦ** www.airboatrentals.com **ⓛ** Open daily 09.00–17.00

Congo River Adventure Golf ★
Congo River Golf offers prizes for great rounds and has live alligators to gawk at. **ⓐ** 4777 Highway 192 (mile marker 12) **ⓣ** 407 396 6900 **ⓦ** www.congoriver.com **ⓛ** Open Sun–Thurs 10.00–23.00, Fri–Sat 10.00–midnight **ⓘ** Admission charge

First Coast Helicopters ★★
Various tours on offer. **ⓐ** 4619 West Irlo Bronson Memorial Highway **ⓣ** 407 390 0111 **ⓘ** Two people minimum

Flying Tigers Warbird Air Restoration Museum ★
Aircraft lovers will feel right at home surrounded by World War II war planes in this family-run museum, where you can watch restoration work on a range of American, British and German planes and have all your questions answered by the knowledgeable guides. Get a tour or

take the controls of a North American T-6 Texan (aka Harvard), the main training aircraft for US pilots in World War II. ⓐ 233 North Hoagland Blvd ⓣ 407 870 7366 ⓦ www.warbirdadventures.com ⓛ Open daily 09.00–17.00 ⓘ Admission charge

Flying Tigers M*A*S*H* Helicopter Tours ★★

Visitors here can take the controls of a beautifully restored Bell 47 helicopter – the classic Vietnam-era chopper – or take the more relaxed approach and let Flying Tigers' pilots do all the work. ⓐ 233 North Hoagland Blvd ⓣ 407 870 7366 ⓦ www.warbirdadventures.com ⓛ Open daily 09.00–17.00

Gatorland ★★★

Unless you are lucky enough to spot one in the wild, the best place to see alligators in Florida is Gatorland. There are hundreds of alligators on show here, from 4.5 m (15 ft) monsters to 20 cm (8 inch) hatchlings, and you can really get a good view of their prehistoric features, gnarled leathery skin and huge teeth. The natural lake behind the main pens has a population of native birds and more than a few free swimming alligators. This gives you the chance to view these animals in as near to wild conditions as is possible. The park is also excellent value for money. ⓐ 14501 Orange Blossom Trail ⓣ 407 855 5496 or 800 393 5297 (freephone in US) ⓦ www.gatorland.com ⓛ Open daily 09.00–17.00 ⓘ Admission charge

Old Town ★★★

Kissimmee's rendition of old town America is one of the most relaxing places to shop but it also offers its fair share of entertainment. You will find eateries and a couple of bars, along with fairground rides for the kids, including a huge Ferris wheel and vintage carousel. Every Friday and Saturday is classic car day with the great 'finned' styling of 1950s Chevrolets and Cadillacs. Catch the action at the Friday Nite Cruise

---

▶ *Getting to grips with the 'gators'*

(vehicles from 1972 to 1987) from 17.00, and the Saturday Cruise, which is in the daytime, from 13.00, with an average of more than 300 cars made earlier than 1972. Thursday nights it is classic bikes – mostly Harley-Davidsons – and on average, more than 700 motorcycles attend! Visitors can chat to the owners and take some great pictures. ➋ 5770 West Irlo Bronson Memorial Highway (3 km/2 miles east of I-4 exit 25) ➊ 407 396 4888 ⓦ www.old-town.com ⓛ Open daily 10.00–21.00, bars open until 23.00 ⓘ Admission free

Reptile World Serpentarium ★

Reptile World provides most of the anti-venom serum that treats victims of snakebite in Florida. You can learn all about this fascinating process and watch snakes being 'milked' of their poison, but the serpentarium also has a great collection of non-venomous species and turtles and lizards for you to view. ⓐ 5705 East Irlo Bronson Highway in St Cloud (34 km/21 miles east of I-4 junction 25) ⓣ 407 892 6905 ⓛ Open Tues–Sun 09.00–17.00 ⓘ Admission charge

SkyCoaster ★

SkyCoaster cranks your specially designed harness 90 m (300 ft) into the air, from where you pull your own ripcord to initiate a spectacular free-fall and long dramatic sway backwards and forwards as you are lowered gently to earth. ⓐ 2850 Florida Plaza Blvd (mile marker 9 off Highway 192, next to Old Town) ⓣ 407 397 2509 ⓛ Open Mon–Fri 16.00–midnight, Sat–Sun noon–midnight ⓘ Admission charge

EVENING ENTERTAINMENT
Arabian Nights ★★★

Voted the number-one dinner attraction by readers of the *Orlando Sentinel* newspaper, this is a great place for children. Many different themed acts from cowboy jamboree and square dancing to Broadway intermingle with the love story of Princess Sheherazade and Prince Kahlid. ⓐ 3081 Arabian Nights Boulevard (Highway 192 east of I-4, at mile marker 8) ⓣ 407 239 9223 ⓦ www.arabian-nights.com ⓛ Open from 17.30 (show starts 19.00) ⓘ Admission charge

Capone's Dinner & Show ★★★

Enter the world of 1920s American prohibition where gangsters ruled the underworld and their molls spent all the loot. An entertaining evening featuring shoot-outs as well as some inter-mob rivalry. ⓐ 4740 West Irlo Bronson Memorial Highway ⓣ 407 397 2378 ⓦ www.alcapones.com ⓛ Open from 19.00 (show starts 19.30) ⓘ Admission charge

Medieval Times ★ ★ ★

Travel back to a time when men wore chain-mail and rode horses, and where honour was proved in contests of jousting, sword-fights, chivalry, agility and strength. This is a great show for all the family. There is a medieval village with numerous artisans to visit while you wait for the performance to start. The roasted meat dinner is hot so watch young children, and you don't get cutlery, so take moist wipes for those after-dinner sticky fingers. ⓐ 4510 West Irlo Bronson Memorial Highway ① 407 396 1518 or 888 935 6878 (freephone in US) ⓦ www.medievaltimes.com ⏱ Open Mon–Fri 18.30 (show starts 19.30), Sat–Sun 18.15 (show starts 19.30) ❶ Admission charge

SHOPPING

Old Town (see page 28) Kissimme's distilled version of old town America is also a relaxing and interesting place to shop. Its approach is very low-key, compared with Disney and Universal, but this is no bad thing. You will find great gifts here that you will not see elsewhere, with rarely a Disney souvenir in sight. Chief amongst them is Americana of all kinds, a surf shop for clothing and equipment, an Irish shop selling themed goods from mugs to CDs of Irish music, and a ghoulish joke shop. ⓐ 5770 West Irlo Bronson Memorial Highway (3 km/2 miles east of I-4 exit 25) ① 407 396 4888 ⏱ Shops open Mon–Sat 10.00–21.00, Sun 10.00–18.00

Osceola Flea and Farmers' Market One of the largest true farmers' markets in the region, you can mix with real local people from the surrounding countryside. This market is a combination of our car boot sales, craft markets and produce markets, and it is certainly interesting to browse even if you do not intend to buy. ⓐ 2801 E Irlo Bronson Memorial Highway ① 407 846 2811 ⏱ Open Fri–Sun 08.00–17.00

RESTAURANTS (see map on page 26)

Bennigan's $–$$ **❶** A great informal family restaurant with a wide range of American dishes on the menu including burgers, salads and steaks. Also open for breakfast. **ⓐ** 5877 West Irlo Bronson Memorial Highway (mile marker 9) **ⓣ** 407 390 0687 **ⓛ** Open daily 08.00–22.00

Pacino's Italian Ristorante $$ **❷** Great American-Italian-style pasta, along with a wide choice of steaks and seafood. **ⓐ** 5795 West Irlo Bronson Memorial Highway **ⓣ** 407 396 8022 **ⓦ** www.pacinos.com **ⓛ** Open daily 11.00–midnight

Ponderosa Steakhouse $$ **❸** Obviously steaks are what Ponderosa do best – they grill them over open flame – although there is plenty more on the menu, including a 'grand buffet' and some great breakfast options. There are three in town. **ⓐ** 4024, 5771, and 7598 West Irlo Bronson Memorial Highway **ⓣ** 407 846 3339/ 397 2100/ 396 7721 **ⓛ** All are open daily 07.00–23.00

Red Lobster $$ **❹** A good family restaurant for seafood. The menu is varied, including options for kids and adults. Obviously lobster is the speciality, but shrimp and catch of the day are tasty too. For non-fish eaters they have steak, chicken and salads. There are two locations in Kissimmee. **ⓐ** 4010 West Vine St (**ⓣ** 407 846 3513/ 5690) and West Irlo Bronson Memorial Highway (**ⓣ** 407 396 6997) **ⓛ** Both are open Sun–Thurs 11.00–22.00, Fri–Sat 11.00–23.00

Tony Roma's $$ **❺** Another Tony Roma's that concentrates on ribs (served with their signature BBQ sauce) but also serves a range of dishes including steak, chicken and seafood platters. **ⓐ** 3415 West Vine St **ⓣ** 407 870 9299 **ⓛ** Open Mon–Fri 11.00–23.00, Sat and Sun 11.00–midnight

Maingate
close to attractions

A part of Kissimmee, Maingate has expanded along the main 192 highway of I-4 junction 25 as the demand for tourist accommodation has grown. It takes its name from its closer proximity to the old Walt Disney World Resort main gate, although it is not right on the doorstep. It is a few miles east of the main Kissimmee attractions.

THINGS TO SEE & DO
Bonanza Mini-Golf ★
The Prospector and Gold Nugget Courses are designed like a set of old mining works and there is a café on site if you want refreshment.
📍 7761 West Irlo Bronson Memorial Highway ☎ 407 396 7536
🕐 Open daily 09.00–midnight

Green Meadows Farm ★★
If you find yourself here with younger kids, the Green Meadows Farm is a certainly one of the area's more charming excursions; more than 300 animals roam freely, and kids can pet and hold many of them including sheep, piglets, donkeys and cows, which can be milked. Horse rides and shows take place all day. 📍 1368 South Poinciana Boulevard ☎ 407 846 0770 🌐 www.greenmeadowsfarm.com
🕐 Tours take place daily from 09.30 to 16.30, farm open until 17.30
ⓘ Admission charge

World of Orchids ★★
For plant lovers, World of Orchids is the perfect place to spend some quality time. These state of the art hot-houses have one of the world's largest collections of this rare tropical flower. Over 2000 specimens are set in different environments. You can also purchase blooms and have them shipped home. 📍 2501 Old Lake Wilson Rd ☎ 407 396 1887
🕐 Open Tues–Sun 09.30–17.30

RESTAURANTS

Angels $$ You will see the adverts for Angels' lobster feast, but keep in mind that this restaurant/buffet serves just about every type of American food and astounding breakfasts – it's the place to take a family that can't agree on what to order. ⓐ 7300 West Irlo Bronson Memorial Highway (at the Holiday Inn) ⓣ 407 397 1960 ⓛ Open daily 07.00–23.00

Giordano's $$ This Italian restaurant specialises in the famous Chicago-style stuffed pizza, but you can also order a variety of pasta dishes, sandwiches and salads ⓐ 7866 West Irlo Bronson Memorial Highway ⓣ 407 397 0044 ⓛ Open daily 11.00–23.30

Outback Steakhouse $$ 'No rules, just right!' is the motto of this Australian-themed eatery. The menu centres on steaks and chicken, but you can get a range of snacks from chicken wings to sandwiches, plus that famed Aussie beer. ⓐ Formosa Gardens, 7804 West Irlo Bronson Memorial Highway ⓣ 407 396 0017 ⓛ Open Sun–Thurs 15.30–22.30, Fri–Sat 15.30–23.30

SHOPPING

Take a trip to **Formosa Gardens** (ⓐ West Irlo Bronson Memorial Highway, mile marker 4), Maingate's principal shopping centre. Although small, it has a select range of shops and restaurants.

Celebration
relax 'small town' style

Truly a 'celebration' of small town America, the way it used to be. This charming, modern settlement has a cosy downtown area designed by Disney with more than a few tributes to the 1950s. Less a resort than a living community, the beautiful lakefront and small shops and restaurants of the centre are surrounded by streets of panel-clad family homes, complete with rocking chairs on the porches. Celebration is probably the most relaxing place to stay in Orlando.

THINGS TO SEE & DO
Carriage rides ★
Take a carriage ride from the lakefront along the main street and view the wonderful homes – no two are the same. ◷ Open 09.00–17.00

Pedalo rides on the lake ★★
Fun for adults and children alike, the pedalos allow you to take to the water at your own pace. ◷ Open 09.00–17.00

Strolling around the lake ★★
Probably the most popular pastime in Celebration. Take your time and say hello to everyone as you pass.

EVENING ENTERTAINMENT
AMC Celebration Theater ★★
For the latest Hollywood releases. ⓐ Front Street ❶ 407 566 1403

RESTAURANTS
Celebration Town Tavern $$$ The Town Tavern has a great reputation for New England seafood including lobster, chowder and fresh fish dishes. ⓐ Lakefront ❶ 407 566 2526 ◷ Open daily 11.00–15.00 and 17.00–22.00

◆ *Creating a splash in Celebration*

Columbia Restaurant $$$ A branch of one of Florida's oldest restaurants, Columbia serves Cuban/Spanish cuisine. It also has an excellent wine list, tapas bar and a cigar bar with fine Dominican cigars. You can dine in the courtyard, adding to the Mediterranean atmosphere. ⓐ Lakefront ⓣ 407 566 1505 ⓛ Open daily 11.30–22.00

Herman's Ice Cream Shoppe $ A delightfully hokey take on an old-fashioned diner/malt shop. ⓐ 671 Front St ⓣ 407 566 1300 ⓛ Open Sun–Thurs 11.00–21.00, Fri–Sat 11.00–22.00

Upper Crust $ Hand-tossed pizzas are the speciality of this New York-style neighbourhood pizzeria. ⓐ Mainstreet ⓣ 407 566 1221 ⓛ Open Sun–Thurs 11.00–21.00, Fri–Sat 11.00–22.00

SHOPPING

Shops in Celebration are scattered along the high street as you find in UK towns, but this is very unusual in the States. The shops are stocked with top-class merchandise and prices are generally higher than in other parts of the city.

Day Dreams Collectable dolls and bears. ⓐ Mainstreet ⓣ 407 566 1231

Hopscotch Classical Ladies clothes, shoes and accessories. ⓐ Mainstreet ⓣ 407 566 2070

Jerrard International Home accessories from around the world. ⓐ Lakefront ⓣ 407 566 2000

Village Mercantile Surfwear and accessories. ⓐ Market Street ⓣ 407 566 0744

ⓐ Directions: I-4, exit 25A onto 192 East (Irlo Bronson Memorial Highway), right at the second set of lights ⓣ 407 566 4900 for information on all activities in the Celebration Marketplace ⓛ All shops are open Mon–Sat 10.00–21.00, Sun noon–18.00

Walt Disney World Resort
a city within a city

Walt Disney World® Resort put Orlando on the tourism map. The theme park that was Walt Disney's personal vision has drawn millions of people each year since it opened in 1971. It has developed far beyond the original plan, with four main parks and several other attractions as well as a range of themed hotels. Today it is almost a city within a city.

TICKET OPTIONS

Disney sells single tickets that are valid for one park, for one day. There is also a whole range of combined tickets that can save money.

Park Hopper tickets allow repeated access to the main parks for as long as the ticket is valid. For example, a four-day Park Hopper allows access for four days.

Park Hopper PLUS tickets give access to the four main parks and a number of other Disney attractions for as long as the ticket is valid. For example, a five-day Park Hopper PLUS gives access to the four main parks plus a choice of two other Disney parks for five days. A six-day Park Hopper PLUS means access to the four main parks and three others for six days. Unused Park Hopper days are still valid for your next visit to Walt Disney World Resort.

Magic Your Way is a new family ticket option with several complex options of days and packages.

At the upper end of the ticketing options, the **World Pass** offers ten days access to all parks, plus a character breakfast. Only the Ultimate Park Hopper ticket offers more choice, but you must stay at a Walt Disney World Resort Hotel to be eligible to buy one.

RESORT DETAILS

For information on all Walt Disney World Resort parks

📞 407 824 4321 🌐 www.disneyworld.com

MAKE THE MOST OF WALT DISNEY WORLD RESORT

- Don't try to do too much. One park per day is a sensible strategy, especially if you have young children.
- Disney is hot and humid year round, and the danger of dehydration is real. Buy 1.5 litre water bottles, which you can refill (free) at any Disney restaurant. Drinks and water in the parks are expensive.
- Hire a pushchair (stroller) for infants because they will become tired.
- If you want to re-enter a park on the same day, have your hand stamped as you leave or they will not let you back in.
- Leave bags in the lockers provided and ask for anything you buy to be delivered to the collection point.
- Use the FASTPASS system. Insert your ticket into the machine at the ride and it will give you a time to return, when you can go on the ride.

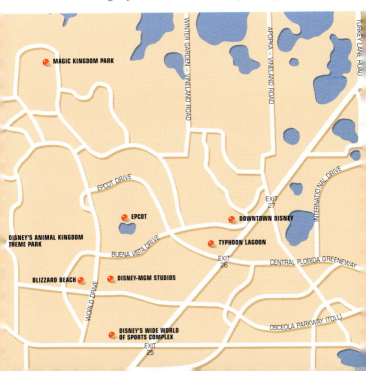

Magic Kingdom Park

Magic Kingdom® Park, the original Disney park in the Walt Disney World Resort, was Walt Disney's personal vision: bringing together the world of Disney cartoons and good old-fashioned fantasy in a riot of colour, song and dance. The park is divided into seven different areas or 'lands'. All radiate from a central sculpture of Walt hand in hand with Mickey Mouse, perhaps his most famous character.

THINGS TO SEE & DO

Adventureland ★★

Hop aboard the **Jungle Cruise**, a journey through lush tropical forest where you will be able to spot wild animals and hidden temples. **Pirates of the Caribbean** highlights the Walt Disney Company's pioneering work with audio-animatronics – figures that move and talk. This exciting attraction is bursting with special effects. **The Magic Carpets of Aladdin** is a great ride for younger children who will love the sensation of flying.

Fantasyland ★★★

If young children could design their own private playground, it would be Fantasyland. The **It's a Small World** ride probably sums up the appeal of the entire area. **Cinderella Castle** is the towering symbol of Fantasyland, if not the whole of Magic Kingdom Park. This abundance of towers and turrets is where the Princess herself presides over **Cinderella's 'Surprise Celebration'** show. Take to the skies in **Peter Pan's Flight** or **Dumbo the Flying Elephant**, ride through **Hundred-Acre Wood** at **The Many Adventures of Winnie the Pooh** or steer the giant teacups at the **Mad Tea Party** fairground ride.

Frontierland ★★★

Themed on the old Wild West, Frontierland has some of the most spectacular rides in Magic Kingdom Park. **Splash Mountain** is based on the 1946 Disney feature *Song of the South*, and is a journey through the land of Brer Rabbit. There is a wonderful surprise finale – be warned, you may get very wet! When you have dried off, head to **Big Thunder Mountain Railroad** – an exhilarating ride in an old carriage running out of control through an abandoned mineshaft.

Liberty Square ★

This is Disney's homage to post-independence USA. Most Americans make time for **The Hall of the Presidents** where audio-animatronic

◀ *Cinderella Castle towers over Magic Kingdom Park* © Disney

re-creations of every American leader tell their tale. If you are a history buff, there is an interesting video on the formulation of the American constitution. Most non-Americans head to the 'ghoulish' surprises of the **Haunted Mansion**.

Main Street, USA ★★★

Just beyond the Magic Kingdom Park entrance, Main Street, USA is one of the best vantage points for the daily **Share A Dream Come True parade**, where all your favourite Disney characters come out to entertain. There is a selection of shops and restaurants, plus information about park activities at City Hall.

Mickey's Toontown Fair ★★

This is the place to meet your favourite classic Disney characters 'in the flesh'. You will find Mr Mouse at home in **Mickey's Country House** and you can tour **Minnie's Country House**, decorated in her own distinctive style. **The Toontown Hall of Fame** brings you up close and personal with Goofy, Pluto and the rest of the gang.

Tomorrowland ★★★

Tomorrowland's appearance is a hi-tech contrast to the sugary pastels of Fantasyland. There is plenty to excite here, including **Space Mountain**, a brilliant covered roller coaster ride that whizzes you across the universe. In **Buzz Lightyear's Space Ranger Spin**, the *Toy Story* character needs your help to win his battle against the evil Emperor Zurg. Older children will also enjoy **ExtraTERRORestrial Alien Encounter**, during which a teleportation accident deposits a pretty scary alien into the heart of the audience. If you fancy a live show, the **Galaxy Palace Theater** productions feature performances by a range of Disney characters.

EVENING ENTERTAINMENT

Fantasy in the Sky ★★★

Finally, bringing the evening to a tumultuous end is the display when Cinderella Castle lights up with a dazzling array of fireworks.

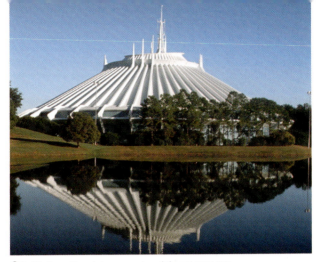

⬤ *Inside Space Mountain you can travel the universe* © Disney

SpectroMagic Parade ★ ★ ★
Takes place twice each night when the park opens late. The cast members' costumes are a mass of sparkling lights.

RESTAURANTS

🍴 **Cinderella's Royal Table** $$$ At Cinderella Castle in Fantasyland Cinderella presides over breakfast, lunch or dinner in the royal hall of her palace. Food 'fit for a king' includes steak, chicken, salads and seafood and is served by costumed waiting staff. ❶ Booking essential

🍴 **Crystal Palace at Main Street, USA** $$ Meet Winnie the Pooh and Tigger too, plus all this friendly bear's other friends at this buffet restaurant. The kids can go and help themselves, which takes the stress out of ordering.

 Pick up a list of the day's activities as soon as you enter the park, so that you can plan your day.

Epcot

Epcot® stands for Experimental Prototype Community of Tomorrow. The park is divided into two separate areas. Future World concentrates on technologies offering the chance to experience themes such as the seas, communication, energy and motion through an array of interactive experiences. World Showcase offers a whistle-stop cultural tour around the planet via 11 country pavilions from all corners of the globe, including the United Kingdom (don't come all the way here and head straight for the pub, though!), Italy, Japan and Germany, among others. The food in this area is excellent.

Epcot is probably the least impressive Disney Park for younger kids, because you do not meet a cartoon character around every corner and it is the most tiring of the parks (twice as big as Magic Kingdom Park). However, older children and adults will enjoy the educational content. Pick up an Epcot guide map at the theme park entrance and time your day around 'must-see' shows. If you want to eat at one of the restaurants, make a reservation, as they can be fully booked by 10.00 during busy periods. The following are some of the highlights in the park.

◆ *Spaceship Earth, Epcot* © Disney

▲ *Test Track at Future World* © Disney

THINGS TO SEE & DO

FUTURE WORLD
Imagination ★★
A theme park would not be a theme park without an exciting ride, so take time to enjoy **Honey, I Shrunk the Audience** when you find yourself miniaturised by mad Professor Szalinski, alias Rick Moranis.

Innoventions East and Innoventions West ★
Much of the technology that Disney has showcased in its two 'Innoventions' sections is now a part of everyday life. Nevertheless, you will still be astonished at what is coming around the corner.

The Land ★★
Take a thought-provoking look at the environment with your hosts Pumbaa, Timon and Simba of *The Lion King* fame in 'Circle of Life'. This explores our relationship with the natural world around us.

The Living Seas ★★★
A huge living coral reef where you can watch a whole ecosystem in action, from the tiniest plankton to the top marine predator, the shark. A new interactive area lets children speak with Crush – the turtle from *Finding Nemo*. Speaking of *Nemo*, kids will also love Bruce's Shark World.

Soarin' ★★★

A hang-gliding journey above the rugged and fertile Californian landscape.

Spaceship Earth ★★

The most photographed building at Future World, Spaceship Earth is a 50 m (164 ft) diameter geodesic dome (or golf ball). The spaceship explores human communication from cave paintings to hi-tech electronic messages.

Test Track ★★★

This is where you can explore the world of the automobile, how they are designed, built and tested – and of course how they are driven. You will be in the front seat on a gruelling and exhilarating simulated vehicle test.

Universe of Energy ★★

Investigate the forces that have ruled our world since the beginning of time. This includes the chance to experience what an earthquake feels like.

Wonders of Life ★★

The Wonders of Life pavilion explores how human beings work. Taking a simulator ride through the human bloodstream to the brain, lungs and heart on **Body Wars** is one of the highlights.

WORLD SHOWCASE
The American Adventure ★★★

The American Adventure is a joyous celebration of all things 'Stateside', including a trip down memory lane as well as the long struggle for independence against the Brits. The whole show is Disney audio-animatronics at its best.

Canada ★★

Canada is the final realm and it features some stunning vistas including recreations of the Rocky Mountain peaks. The film *O Canada!* does real justice to its wonderful varied landscape.

China ★★

New here is the interesting Hong Kong Disneyland preview center, where you can get a taste of what Disney's newest international park will feature.

France ★★

France lies in the shadow of a replica Eiffel Tower. The *Impressions of France* is one of the best film productions of World Showcase, and of course the food here is sublime.

Mexico ★★

Mexico is housed in an impressive recreation of a Mayan pyramid, where the **El Rio del Tiempo** river ride takes you on a journey through Mexican history.

Norway ★★★

This pavilion features the best ride in World Showcase – **Maelstrom**. Combining a scenic tour of Scandinavia with some historical background, you find yourself caught up in a North Sea storm, falling off the edge of a waterfall.

EVENING ENTERTAINMENT

IllumiNations: Reflections of Earth ★★★

A riot of lasers, fireworks and music plays across the lake in a brilliant 15-minute climax to the activities of the day.

RESTAURANTS

The Sunshine Season Food Fair $ This is a selection of stalls which sell snacks from all the countries featured in World Showcase. There is bound to be something here for every family member!

Coral Reef Restaurant $$$ Watch the graceful progress of sharks, rays and huge barracuda, separated from their world by a strong wall of plexi-glass. Fish is on the menu here, but it is not caught on site!

Disney's Animal Kingdom Theme Park

The success of the Disney film *The Lion King* sparked off the idea for this newest realm of the Disney family, where real, live animals from around the world are featured. Of course, Disney has pepped up the whole experience with rides, parades and razzmatazz. A boring zoo this ain't!

THINGS TO SEE & DO

Africa ★★

This recreation of the vast African plains is the anchor for Disney's Animal Kingdom Theme Park. **Kilimanjaro Safaris** allows you to enter this

Prepare to get wet on the Kali River Rapids © Disney

world for close encounters with elephants, giraffes and ostriches. Walk along the **Pangani Forest Exploration Trail** where you can watch the cheeky antics of gorillas, or get an underwater view of a hippo. Take the train to **Rafiki's Planet Watch**, for an introduction to wildlife conservation.

Asia ★★

Step into the imaginary world of Anandapur and walk the **Maharajah Jungle Trek** to meet gibbons, tapirs and view the king of the Asian cats in their 2 ha (5 acre) **Tiger Range**. Take in the **Flights of Wonder** bird show, where vultures, eagles and others show off their flying skills. On **Kali River Rapids** you are guaranteed to get wet, so be prepared.

In **Expedition Everest**, you'll ride on a single-line track through Himalayan countryside. Look over the edge to see the 25 m (80 ft) drop!

Camp Minnie-Mickey ★★

This is classic Walt Disney Theme Park stuff, with a series of Disney Character Greetings Trails where you will meet your favourite cartoon characters. There is a spectacular stage extravaganza **Festival of The Lion King** and children will enjoy the **Pocahontas and Her Forest Friends** show. Here, woodland animals help Pocahontas to save their forest home.

DinoLand USA ★★★

DinoLand has the park's most exciting ride, **Dinosaur** – asteroids fall from the skies and there is a T-Rex around every corner. At **The Boneyard** you can let the kids climb on life-size recreations of dinosaur skeletons and, if you still have energy left, get with the beat at **Tarzan Rocks!** – a live concert featuring the best Disney film songs.

Discovery Island ★★

At the heart of Disney's Animal Kingdom Theme Park is the 61 m (200 ft) tall **Tree of Life**, its trunk carved with hundreds of animals. You will find most of the restaurants and shops around it, along with **It's Tough to be a Bug!** – a hilarious look at the world through an insect's eyes. You will also get a great view of **Mickey's Jammin' Jungle Parade**.

RESTAURANT

Rainforest Café at the Oasis $$ An amazing restaurant that recreates a rainforest environment. Audio-animatronic animals add to the authentic effect. Menu includes steaks, chicken and sandwiches.

For the best view of the animals, it is best to visit this park early or late in the day – the animals take to the shade in the midday sun, and so will be harder to see at this time.

Disney-MGM Studios

Not just a theme park, but a real-life working film studio. Disney-MGM Studios takes you to the heart of the action, yet still manages to provide some of the best rides of any of the Disney parks. Here is your opportunity to take a journey through movie land, from Disney's point of view.

THINGS TO SEE & DO
Animation Courtyard ★
The Magic of Disney Animation gives this small area its name – a fascinating film exploring the art of cartoon making, with clips from many

⬤ *Catastrophe Canyon* © Disney

Disney classics. **Playhouse Disney – Live On Stage!** is a show for under-fives featuring characters from American TV. British children may not recognise many of them, but **Voyage of The Little Mermaid** brings the instantly recognizable Princess Ariel's world to life through cast members, puppets and special effects.

Behind the Scenes Tour ★★★

The Disney-MGM studios Behind the Scenes Tour is a three-stage attraction where you get the chance to see how movies are made. **The Backstage Pass Tour** shows real-life productions taking shape at the studio soundstages.

Disney Stars and Motor Cars Parade ★

A daily procession of amazing 'morphed' vehicles carrying the stars of your favourite Disney films.

Hollywood Boulevard and Sunset Boulevard ★★★

These two streets form the heart of the shopping and eating opportunities within the park. The far end of Sunset Boulevard has some of the best rides and shows. The huge skyscraper at the end of the street is **The Twilight Zone Tower of Terror**, a ride through an abandoned and haunted hotel, which incorporates many special effects used in *The Twilight Zone* paranormal TV series. Disney's first inverted ride, **Rock 'n' Roller Coaster Starring Aerosmith**, takes you on a fantastic 3D ride through Disney's Los Angeles, with rock group Aerosmith providing the soundtrack. For live entertainment, **Beauty and the Beast – Live on Stage** recreates the highlights of this hit Disney movie. Over on Hollywood Boulevard you will find **Walt Disney – One Man's Dream**, all about the man himself. It is great background knowledge for movie fans. There is a cavalcade of audio-animatronic stars at **The Great Movie Ride** recreating some great MGM film moments, from Gene Kelly in *Singing in the Rain* to the monster from *Alien*. **Star Tours** highlights the realm of George Lucas films and features a spectacular trip in a Star Speeder – zooming through space on that famous route through the alleyways of the Death Star. The **Indiana Jones Epic Stunt Spectacular!** takes you from hi-tech to good old-fashioned swashbuckling action where the explorer's greatest action sequences are replayed – with real-life actors taking all the risks. Similar neck-risking can be seen at **Lights! Motors! Action!**, an extreme stunt show including cars, motorcycles, and watercraft soaring through and above a village in a Mediterranean setting. The **Sound Stage Experience** lets you walk through a behind-the-scenes look at the making of *The Chronicles of Narnia*.

Mickey Avenue ★ ★ ★

Mickey Avenue is home to a varied collection of attractions. Head to **Who Wants To Be A Millionaire – Play It!** if you want to sit in the hot seat and answer the $1 million question just like they do on TV. You will not win cash, but there are Disney goods for the best scores. The Disney-MGM Studios Backlot Tour, featuring **Catastrophe Canyon**, enters the world of special effects and tours parts of the studios that are off-limits to the public. Finally, you explore a gallery of movie costumes and props from hit productions.

New York Street ★ ★

At **Jim Henson's MuppetVision 3D** you dive into the chaos and hoopla of the Muppet Theater, where Kermit, Miss Piggy and Fozzie Bear really do look as though they are just in front of you, and the antics never stop.

EVENING ENTERTAINMENT
Fantasmic! ★ ★ ★

Features Mickey Mouse in his role as the Sorcerer's Apprentice whose dreams take on a fantastic life of their own. It is entertainment on an epic scale, a true stage spectacular.

RESTAURANT

The Sci-Fi Dine-In Theater Restaurant $$ A mock drive-in where you are served by waitresses on roller skates and you can watch non-stop black and white sci-fi film clips as you eat.

Best of the rest

In the last few years, Walt Disney World Resort has grown far beyond Walt's own vision. Here are some highlights to choose from after you have enjoyed the main resort parks. Remember though that each of the following has its own admission charge and/or parking charges.

Disney's Blizzard Beach Water Park ★★

Only Disney would consider creating a water-park themed on a ski resort, but Blizzard Beach is exactly that – a series of adventure 'zones' where the rides are all styled as ski, toboggan and bob-sleigh runs. Towering above is snow-capped Mount Gushmore – at 27.5 m (90 ft) it is the world's tallest free-fall flume. You can even take a chair-lift to the top for great views over the park. ❸ 1801 West Buena Vista Drive, Lake Buena Vista ❶ 1800 W DISNEY or 407 824 2222

Disney's Typhoon Lagoon ★★

One of the first Disney water-parks and the one many still consider the best, Typhoon Lagoon is themed on the aftermath of a tropical storm. Amongst the wooden shacks, flotsam and jetsam you will find a huge surf pool with perfect 1.5 m (5 ft) waves, surrounded by a wonderful fine sand beach and hammocks to laze the afternoon away. **Humunga Kowabunga** is a three-flume slide chute and there are body-slides, rafting courses and **Katchakiddee Creek** with activities especially for the two- to six-year-olds. **Crush'n Gusher** is a new water coaster. You can also snorkel in a huge salt-water reef with rays, fish and real sharks (though not the ones that eat humans). ❸ Near Pleasure Island and the AMC Theater along Buena Vista Drive ❶ 407 560 4141

Disney's Wide World of Sports Complex ★

Disney's homage to the American love of sports is probably the least interesting attraction in the whole Walt Disney World Resort to football-loving Brits. However, this complex is state of the art, can cater to over 30 different sports and is beginning to attract some high-class sporting tournaments. ❷ Walt Disney World Resort ❶ 407 824 2222 or 800 W DISNEY (freephone in US) ◷ Closed winter

Richard Petty Driving Experience ★

After all the roller coasters, water chutes and interactive games, the Richard Petty Driving Experience brings a thrilling touch of high-speed reality to Disney. Visitors here can enjoy the thrill of the 1.5 km (1 mile) oval racetrack in the capable hands of the professional drivers. ❷ Walt Disney World Speedway at the Magic Kingdom Park ❶ 407 939 0130 Ⓦ www.1800bepetty.com ❶ Reservations required

⬇ *Watch out for the real sharks in Disney's Typhoon Lagoon!* © Disney

Downtown Disney

Although some of the Disney parks stay open late, the resort also has a purpose-built entertainment area that comes into its own as night falls. Downtown Disney® brings together restaurants, nightclubs, cinemas and live music venues, and it hosts some of the most unusual shopping opportunities in Orlando. Downtown Disney is divided into three distinct areas, each with its own highlights: Downtown Disney West Side, Pleasure Island and Marketplace.

THINGS TO SEE & DO

Cirque du Soleil ★ ★ ★

A wonderful aerial spectacle, the Cirque du Soleil show 'La Nouba' is a celebration of the acrobatic and gymnastic arts. Other circus acts are also held in this state of the art 'big-top'-style arena. ☎ 407 939 7600

DisneyQuest Indoor Interactive Theme Park ★ ★

A five-storey techno-park where you can try your hand at any number of virtual diversions, including cutting your own CD. Head for the internet café or try retro computer games such as Asteroids.

RESTAURANTS

DOWNTOWN DISNEY WEST SIDE

Bongos Cuban Café $$ Emilio and Gloria Estefan own this informal restaurant, which serves excellent and delicious Cuban food. As you would expect, the Latin music is great.

RESORT DETAILS

ⓐ Downtown Disney I-4 exit 26B ☎ 407 WDW 2NITE (939 2648)
ⓦ www.downtowndisney.com
For all dining options at the resort ☎ 407 WDW-DINE (939 3463)

Planet Hollywood $$ This is the largest restaurant in the Planet Hollywood chain. There is some interesting memorabilia and a good range of food, from sandwiches to steaks.

PLEASURE ISLAND

Fulton's Crab House $$ A floating restaurant styled like an old river-steamer. As you would expect, the menu leans heavily to seafood.

🔺 *Celebrations at Pleasure Island* © Disney

Rainforest Café $$ A café themed on a tropical rainforest sounds silly, but these eateries are wonderfully done with an authentic forest soundtrack and audio-animatronic animals.

NIGHTLIFE

DOWNTOWN DISNEY WEST SIDE
House of Blues Based on the *Blues Brothers* film, this concert hall comes alive every night with a range of sounds from blues to rock to soul.

PLEASURE ISLAND
Pleasure Island has the main concentration of nightclub and live music venues in Downtown Disney. There is a separate charge after dark and some age restrictions apply.

8TRAX Transports you back to the 1970s with non-stop hits from the era of bell-bottoms.

Adventurers' Club Watch the antics of a range of inventive cast members.

The BET Soundstage Club Showcases the latest in hip hop and R&B. Comedy Warehouse improvised stand-up routines come thick and fast.

Mannequin's Dance Palace With its revolving dance floor, this club has been voted the best dance venue in the US.

Motion Mainstream pop.

Pleasure Island Jazz Company Try this club for a little syncopation.

Raglan Road This is a new Irish pub.

Rock 'n Roll Beach Club Rock classics.

MARKETPLACE

Marketplace is the main shopping section of Downtown Disney, with a range of individual stores that you will not find elsewhere in Orlando.

 Art of Disney If you are into cartoon memorabilia, including original cartoon 'cells', then this is the shop for you. These are unique pieces and priced accordingly.

Lego Imagination Center This interactive playground and shop will keep children happy for hours, and there is an excellent range of Lego kits to buy.

World of Disney The anchor store of Marketplace, this is also the largest Disney store in the world. You are bound to find just what you need.

Universal Orlando Resort
impressive experience

Universal Orlando® Resort is situated just off International Drive and I-4 and encompasses two huge side-by-side theme parks, Universal Studios Florida and Islands of Adventure. A 30-acre entertainment park, CityWalk, doubles as a gateway to both theme parks.

Orlando was the natural location for Universal to build a theme park based on their blockbuster hit films. Disney's roller coasters and 3-D rides just don't stack up against the Universal experience – Universal Studios Florida, which opened in 1990, was an immediate success, with the best rides, in this ride-packed town. In 1999 Universal opened Islands of Adventure, considered the most complete theme park experience in the world. Who could fail to be impressed with Steven Spielberg as creative consultant? Also opened in 1999, and linking the two, CityWalk provides a huge variety of restaurants, themed restaurants, nightclubs, state-of-the-art cinemas and live entertainment venues.

⏷ All aboard for the best rides in town

Universal Studios Florida

While the Universal Studios Florida® theme park appeals more to older children and adults than to young kids, the park attempts to entertain young ones with a special section just for them. The park is divided into themed areas surrounding an artificial lake where you can take boat rides or enjoy a meal at one of a range of restaurants.

THINGS TO SEE & DO

HOLLYWOOD
Lucy: A Tribute ★
Fantastic fun for fans of the *I Love Lucy* TV series, with classic shows, scripts and costumes.

Terminator 2: 3-D Battle Across Time ★★★
Based on the hugely successful Hollywood blockbuster, this 'part show, part film' puts you in the heart of the action. A Cyberdyne Systems demonstration is hijacked and you travel into the future to watch John and his Terminator protector attempt to save the world. The original cast and director filmed 12 minutes of extra footage purely for this attraction, and it cost more to shoot than the original *Terminator 2* film, but was definitely worth it. The 3-D effects are spectacular and it's well worth seeing.

Universal Horror Make-Up Show: Revenge of The Mummy ★
Teenagers and adults will be fascinated by this film which shows just how actors are turned into scary monsters or mutilated victims.

NEW YORK
The Blues Brothers ★★
Jake and Elwood Blues (well, not the real guys) get together daily to perform a selection of hits from their film. It is great entertainment, but even better if you have seen the film and can sing along.

Twister – Ride It Out ★★

Based on the hit film, this attraction recreates a little of what it feels like to encounter a tornado – obviously it is not as bad as the real thing!

PRODUCTION CENTRAL

Just beyond the entrance to the park, Production Central has all the guest service facilities. This is where you sign up to be in the audience of any TV productions that are taking place that day.

Jimmy Neutron's Nicktoon Blast ★★★

Jimmy's friend Carl and his robot dog, Goddard, invite everyone to help Jimmy recover his stolen rocket and save the planet from scoundrel villain Ooblar. On the way, *The Fairly OddParents*, *The Rugrats* and *SpongeBob SquarePants* add more fun to this frantic simulator ride.

Nickelodeon Studios ★

Nickelodeon is the number-one American TV network for kids and it is here that the programmes are made. Definitely one for the under-tens.

Shrek 4-D ★★★

Mindblowing digital show with surprising and innovative sensory elements. OgreVision glasses and specially designed seats make everyone part of the new adventures of Shrek, Fiona and Donkey. One of the best new shows in Orlando.

SAN FRANCISCO/AMITY
Beetlejuice's Rock 'n' Roll Graveyard Revue ★★

A musical spectacular bringing together a gruesome collection of performers from Frankenstein to the Wolfman.

Earthquake – The Big One ★★★

Initially, the attraction spends time explaining how the special effects for the film were achieved, before you get to find out just what it feels like to live through an earthquake. As you travel through the San Francisco

⬥ *Lookout – behind you!*

subway, the earthquake begins. Then the tunnel collapses, fires explode around you and you begin to get a sense of the terror involved.

Jaws ★ ★ ★
Just when you thought it was safe to go back on another ride you reach Amity, and your quiet boat trip becomes a fight for survival as the 10 m (32 ft) shark wants you for his next meal.

WOODY WOODPECKER'S KIDZONE
If some of the rides at Universal prove too scary for small children, Woody Woodpecker's Kidzone is a place where they are sure to feel at home. There is plenty to enjoy, and a few familiar characters to meet along the way including Woody himself, Barney the dinosaur and ET.

Animal Planet Live! ★ ★
A number of rescue animals and old animal film stars from Universal pictures appear on stage, showing off a range of stunts and helped by a few small members of the audience.

Curious George Goes To Town ★ ★
An action-packed playground that includes water games.

A Day In The Park With Barney ★ ★
The only place on earth where kids can meet this friendly purple dinosaur, and he hosts his own stage show with lots of sing-along children's songs.

ET Adventure ★ ★
Head out over the imaginary treetops at ET Adventure where you follow everyone's favourite alien on your flying bikes. A pleasant journey with glorious scenery, though thrill seekers may find it a little tame.

Fievel's Playland ★
The cartoon mouse invites children to get physical with themed climbing frames, slides and trampolines.

Woody Woodpecker's Nuthouse Coaster ★★

This is the answer to those frustrating height restrictions on the larger rides. Anyone over 1 m (3 ft) can ride, and though it goes slowly compared with adult rides, it divides kids into two camps – those who want to ride over and over, and those who will never try a roller coaster again.

WORLD EXPO

Back To The Future: The Ride ★★★

You have to go back in time to stop bad boy Biff from changing the time-line. Strap yourself into your De Lorean time machine and prepare for the simulator ride of a lifetime – the graphics are just amazing and all the more realistic on the huge wraparound screen!

Men in Black – Alien Attack ★★★

Do you want to save the earth from aliens? As a trainee agent you head off on the adventure of a lifetime, zapping monsters with your ray gun. Unfortunately the aliens shoot back and you need to get a better score than them in order to save the earth. It is like being in the middle of a huge computer game and the plot changes, depending on how skilled you are, so you may not have the same ride twice.

RESTAURANTS

Finnegan's Bar and Grill $$ Familiar dishes include shepherds pie and corn-beef hash in this New York-style eatery, with more than a leaning towards the Emerald Isle. ❷ At New York

Lombard's Seafood Grille $$ Overlooking the inner lagoon, Lombard's Landing is the largest eatery at Universal Studios and offers a choice of seafood, salads and sandwiches. ❷ At San Francisco/Amity

Mel's Drive-In $ Burgers, hot dogs and milk shakes in this 1950s-style diner themed on the one in the film *American Graffiti* starring Richard Gere. ❷ At Hollywood

Islands of Adventure

Universal's second theme park, Islands of Adventure®, is next to Universal Studios Florida and is rated as the most complete theme park in Orlando, which is saying something when you look at the competition. There are attractions for all members of the family here and more thrilling five-star rides than any other park, for those who need that adrenalin rush! The park is divided into five themed islands, connected by bridges circled around the lake, and the Port of Entry with its shops and restaurants.

THINGS TO SEE & DO

JURASSIC PARK

Step into the world of *Jurassic Park*, the film, to find many different experiences, all with a prehistoric theme.

Camp Jurassic ★★

A perfect playground for mini-dinosaur hunters, including an 'active' volcano to explore.

Jurassic Park Discovery Center ★★★

Watch a baby dinosaur hatch, or mix your DNA with a dinosaur in a computer simulation – just two of the interactive exhibits here.

Jurassic Park River Adventure ★★★

The theme for this ride is a river journey through the landscape of the Cretaceous period. You catch glimpses of raptors in the undergrowth – but where is the T-Rex? Be ready to make a dramatic escape!

Pteranodon Flyers ★★★

Youngsters can fly over Jurassic Park, carried by giant pteranodons. Riders must be 1–1.5 m (3–4 ft, 8 inches) tall or be accompanied by a height-qualified rider.

Triceratops Discovery Trail ★

An interesting display of dino-animatronics aimed at the young ones, where they will be given the opportunity to visit one of several 'feed and control' paddocks and maybe even pet a dinosaur.

THE LOST CONTINENT

If many Jurassic Park attractions have a pseudo-scientific feel, the Lost Continent is pure fantasy. Universal's twist on Atlantis, the World of 1001 Knights and a host of other legendary lands.

Duelling Dragons ★★★

A roller coaster with a difference. There are two inverted roller coasters and through a series of twists, loops and one 30.5 m (100 ft) drop, you come tantalisingly close to collision with the other group of riders – at speeds of nearly 90 km/h (55 mph).

The Eighth Voyage of Sinbad ★★

Follow the adventures of Sinbad and his sidekick as they rescue Princess Amoura from the clutches of evil witch Miseria. This live show has some good special effects and the cast pull off some energetic stunts.

Flying Unicorn ★

A junior-sized roller coaster ride for six- to 12-year-olds.

Poseidon's Fury: Escape from the Lost City ★★★

Enter Poseidon's underwater realm in this walk-through multimedia attraction. Features a fantastic final duel scene between Zeus, armed with fire, and Poseidon, armed with water.

MARVEL SUPER HERO ISLAND

This is where the heroes step out of the pages of Marvel Comics to meet and greet – lots of opportunities for photo sessions.

◗ *Meet your favourite superhero*

The Amazing Adventures of Spider-Man ★★★

An audio-visual spectacular puts you in the heart of the battle between Spider-Man, alias ace reporter Peter Parker, and his arch-enemies. With the 3-D effects and the motion simulator, you will feel every move that 'Spidey' makes, including a drop off a skyscraper that leaves your stomach in your mouth.

Doctor Doom's Fearfall ★★

One minute you are sitting on the ground, the next you are heading skyward at breakneck speed to the top of the 61 m (200 ft) tower with a view over much of Orlando. A quick ride, but very exhilarating.

Incredible Hulk Coaster ★★★

If it's a Hulk Coaster, then it's got to be big and dramatic. This roller coaster heads out over Islands of Adventure lagoon at speeds of up to 105 km/h (65 mph), turning you every which way.

Storm Force Accelatron ★

This milder fairground-style ride, with special effects, caters to young visitors.

SEUSS LANDING

Enter the kooky world of Dr Seuss, where everything rhymes and there are no straight lines. Most kids will know *The Grinch* cartoon film and he is just one of many characters here. A magnet for the under fives.

Caro-Seuss-el ★

An old-fashioned carousel ride with Seuss characters instead of horses.

The Cat In The Hat ★★

Ride through the story of *The Cat in the Hat*. Your coaster takes you up and around the slinky Seuss animals.

If I Ran The Zoo ★

An interactive play park with lots of activities, most of which seem to include getting wet.

One Fish, Two Fish, Red Fish, Blue Fish ★

This fairground-style ride is a great hit with young riders. You must make

---

 The Incredible Hulk Coaster

the Seuss-style fish travel up and down in time with the music. If you fail, you get fired on from mini-water cannons.

TOON LAGOON

Enter the world of comic hero Popeye for a series of 'watery' experiences.

Dudley Do-Right's Ripsaw Falls ★★
Another option for a soaking, this time an 18 m (60 ft) drop is part of the action (set to re-open in April 2006).

Me Ship, The Olive ★
Popeye's boat is full of interactive games for small kids. Best of all you can fire water at the people passing on Bilge Rat Barges.

Popeye and Bluto's Bilge-Rat Barges ★★
If Popeye organizes a boat trip you just know that you are going to get very wet. It is not just the waves and waterfalls: you will be attacked from the banks by water cannon.

RESTAURANTS

Green Eggs and Ham Café $ Try the meal of the same name, invented by Dr Seuss himself – and yes the eggs are green!
Ⓐ At Seuss Landing

Mythos Restaurant $$ Styled as the inside of a dormant volcano, you eat amongst underground waterfalls and lava plumes. Serves good quality steak, chicken, pizza, and seafood. Ⓐ At The Lost Continent

UNIVERSAL ORLANDO RESORT DETAILS
Ⓐ 1000 Universal Boulevard ☏ 407 363 8000
Ⓦ www.universalorlando.com ⏰ Open daily 09.00–18.00 (later in summer; CityWalk 11.00–23.00) ❶ Admission charge

Universal CityWalk

Universal's latest attraction takes the excitement into the evening hours. This entertainment village combines shopping, dining, live performances and the latest silver screen epics. Though it is open during the day
(it links the two Universal theme parks and is a popular place for lunch and snacks), the atmosphere of Universal CityWalk® is more highly charged after nightfall. Age restrictions apply to enter nightclubs.

RESTAURANTS & BARS

 Emeril's Restaurant Orlando $$$ Famed New Orleans chef Emeril Lagasse brings his Cajun-influenced menu and impeccable Continental-style service to Universal. This is one place to really push the boat out. ☎ 407 224 2424 ⏰ Open Sun–Thurs 11.30–14.00, 17.30–22.00, Fri–Sat 11.30– 14.00, 17.30–23.00 ❶ Reservations recommended

 Hard Rock Café $$ The world's largest Hard Rock Café, with interesting memorabilia and great music. ⏰ Open daily 11.00–late

Jimmy Buffet's Margaritaville $$ The musician and native Floridian Jimmy Buffet owns this bar/diner. Laidback island style is the influence, with lots of seafood, salads and pasta on the menu. Live music or Jimmy's own. ⏰ Open daily 11.00–late

Nascar Café $ Themed on the Nascar racing formula, there are real cars outside for you to admire and races on TV inside. Menu includes burgers, chicken and ribs. ⏰ Open daily 11.00–late

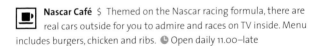 **Orlando Palm** $$$ The same family have owned the upmarket Palm restaurants chain since 1926 and this eatery, the latest in the stable, is already a hit with Orlando natives as well as with visitors. Signature dishes are excellent steaks and chops, although you can also

choose from a range of seafood dishes. Excellent wine list. ⓐ 5800 Universal Blvd at the Hard Rock Hotel ☎ 407 503 7256 ⏰ Open daily 17.00–late ❶ Reservations recommended

Pastamoré Ristoranté & Market $$ This is a casual, family-style Italian restaurant and an outdoor market place café ⓐ 1000 Universal Studios Plaza ☎ 407 224 4663 ⏰ Open daily 17.00–midnight, café 08.00–02.00

NIGHTLIFE

Bob Marley: A tribute to freedom The recreation of Bob Marley's Jamaican home is the setting for great live reggae music and the restaurant serves jerk pork and chicken. ⏰ Open daily 14.00–02.00

Cityjazz Combines a tribute to the great jazz icons with a venue for the latest in live jazz. Tapas bar. ⏰ Open daily 20.00–02.00

the groove Disco/club with the latest dance music, 70s night, 80s disco and teen night on Fridays. ⏰ Open daily 21.00–02.00

Hard Rock Live Concert venue for mid- to big-name musicians; see the schedule at ⓦ www.hardrocklive.com

Latin Quarter The latest Latin sounds with guest DJs or live bands, along with great spicy South American food. ⏰ Open Mon–Fri 17.00–02.00, Sat–Sun noon–02.00

Motown Café Classic soul and a live tribute band. Full service restaurant and 1970s-style drinking lounge. ⏰ Open Sun–Thurs 11.30–16.00 and 11.30–23.00 ❶ Cover charge after 21.00

SeaWorld
aquatic antics

One of the world's leading aquatic theme parks, SeaWorld is both an entertainment centre and education facility, offering exciting animal shows, attention-grabbing exhibits and the chance to find out more about how you can help to save the world's oceans. Now owned by brewing giant Anheuser-Busch, which has spared no expense on environments for the animals or human guests, there are two new rides to rival those of Disney and Universal for excitement and exhilaration.

THINGS TO SEE & DO

Blue Horizons ★★

Dolphins, false killer whales and exotic birds including blue and gold macaws, sun conures and an Andean condor cavort above and below the water.

Clyde and Seamore take Pirate Island ★★

A hilarious show featuring playful sea lions and a cheeky otter. The pre-show mime is well worth seeing. At the Sea Lion and Otter Stadium. After the show see a whole collection of sea lions and walruses with their own wave machine recreating their natural breakwater environment. Pacific Point Reserve.

Journey to Atlantis ★★★

SeaWorld's water-coaster ride takes you on a voyage to a lost world, with many damp adventures en-route, and one dramatic drenching. The special effects and audio-visuals are extremely impressive.

THEME PARK DETAILS
ⓐ 7007 SeaWorld Drive, off International Dr ☎ 407 363 2613
ⓦ www.seaworld.com ⏱ Open 09.00–19.00 (later in summer)

 The manatee pool at SeaWorld

Key West at SeaWorld ★ ★ ★
The dolphins play in their vast sea water pool – Dolphin Cove. There are several feeding times during the day when the dolphins will come and take fish from your hand. The Key West Dolphin Fest show takes place at the nearby stadium. Key West also has Turtle Point and Stingray Lagoon, where you can hand-feed these unusual flat fish.

Kraken ★ ★ ★
Kraken is the longest, fastest and highest ride in Orlando. You dangle (safely of course) from a 'floorless mega-coaster' and so the ride feels even more thrilling.

Manatee Rescue ★ ★
Manatees, also known as sea cows, are gentle slow-moving creatures that graze on vegetation on the coastal shallows and inter-coastal waterways. You can watch these endangered mammals from above and below the water, and learn about programmes to protect them in the wild.

Odyssea ★ ★
A unique, 30 minute underwater-themed circus and acrobatics exhibition.

Penguin Encounter ★★

Penguins 'do their thing', totally oblivious to the audience on the other side of the viewing screen. Look out for the baby penguins – they look just like the fluffy bearskin busbies worn by the guards outside Buckingham Palace.

Orlando Flexticket allows 14 days unlimited access to Universal Studios Florida, Orlando Universal's Islands of Adventure, SeaWorld and Wet 'n Wild. Add Busch Gardens for $35 more.

Pets Ahoy ★★

A funny show featuring a variety of small animals, from dogs to pot-bellied pigs, most of them from rescue homes. At the SeaWorld Theater.

Shamu Stadium ★★★

Although SeaWorld is now far more than the killer whale show that originally made it famous, Shamu and his relatives are still probably the most popular attractions in the park. These huge mammals perform graceful manoeuvres in the large display pool, but everyone really comes for the finale when their huge tails splash water out into the auditorium soaking everyone in the lower seats. Kids just love it! Parents – protect your cameras from the salt water.

Skytower ★★★

You get a fantastic panorama of greater Orlando plus great sunsets from this 120 m (400 ft) viewing platform (extra charge).

ACTIVITIES

SeaWorld runs several interactive programmes including an **Animal Care Experience**, **False Killer Whale Interaction programme**, and a **Trainer for a Day programme** (extra charge). These need to be booked well in advance. ☎ 407 370 1382 🌐 www.seaworld.com

Wild Arctic ★★★

Take a simulated helicopter ride over this frozen landscape to the 'research station' at Base Arctic Wild. Here you will see the inhospitable environment that the polar bear, walruses and Beluga whales call home.

If you want VIP treatment at SeaWorld, book the Adventure Express Tour (extra charge). You will have a personal guide, priority access to rides, seats at the shows and opportunities to feed the animals.

RESTAURANT

Mango Joe's Café $ A delicious range of sandwiches, including hot offerings of beef, chicken and fish, also Mexican fajitas, salads and numerous side items. ❸ Near Shamu Stadium and Wild Arctic

🔺 *Get soaked by Shamu at SeaWorld*

Discovery Cove
dolphin delights

Discovery Cove, a sister attraction to SeaWorld, recreates a desert island hideaway. Here, you can spend a day away from the crowds and hi-tech theme parks and relax on soft white beaches or swim in teeming waters. Not only that, but there is the opportunity to swim with a dolphin – you cannot do that anywhere else in Orlando.

Discovery Cove aims to offer an exclusive experience, which means that the 12 ha (30 acres) of lush landscaped park is open to just 1000 people each day. It is the most expensive adventure park in the city and reservations in advance are required, but you are guaranteed few queues, lots of space and a very personal service. Think of it as a five-star resort without

◆ *Swim like a ray*

THEME PARK DETAILS

ⓐ Entrance next to the Central Florida Parkway ☎ 877 434 7268
ⓦ www.discoverycove.com

the hotel room and you'll get the right idea. There is a high staff-to-guest ratio and the staff make plenty of time to answer all your questions.

You will be given towels, snorkel, goggles and flippers to use. There are wet suits in case you find the 26°C (80°F) water cold (you need to wear this or a Discovery Cove life jacket while in the water for safety purposes) and there are buoyancy aids for poor swimmers. A decent lunch is also included in the price (other snacks are reasonably priced). The park has been divided into a number of different environments.

 Admission to Discovery Cove also provides seven days unlimited access to SeaWorld. See website for details.

THINGS TO SEE & DO
Aviary ★★

Part of the tropical river section leads into the aviary, and you can also reach it on foot along the beach. There is an interesting and varied collection of tropical birds, including peacocks, which are housed amongst trees within a high net boundary that lets in lots of light and fresh air. At feeding time the cheeky ones fly to your hand for a snack.

Coral Reef ★★★

Filled with thousands of tropical fish and monster-sized rays lounging on the bottom, this huge pool recreates a coral marine environment. Swim around the remains of a wooden boat 'shipwrecked' here. Although the coral is not real you will be amazed at the sheer numbers of jack fish and angelfish – they swarm around you at feeding time (some young children may find this a little disconcerting). The predators are at one end of the reef, separated from the fish and human visitors by a sheet of strong

● *Get up close and personal during the Dolphin Swim*

plexi-glass. Look through it to see the sharks and barracuda swimming around on the look-out for their next meal.

The Dolphin Swim ★★★

Undoubtedly the highlight of your day at Discovery Cove (extra charge), the dolphin encounter allows you to get up close and personal with one of the most intelligent and thought-provoking creatures on the planet. When you book in at Discovery Cove you will be given a time for your Dolphin Swim. You receive a 15-minute introductory session before you enter the dolphin lagoon and, once in the water, one of the very professional animal trainers, who make both the humans and the dolphins feel at ease, will guide you. Group sizes range from six to 12 but everyone gets to have their photograph taken and play with one of these delightful mammals. It's a good idea to wear a wet suit for your encounter, as the water is colder than you think and you will spend well over 15 minutes being fairly inactive while you wait your turn.

Ray Lagoon ★★

Next door to the coral reef, this lagoon is full of small- to medium-sized rays. You can attempt to emulate their graceful movement through the water.

Tropical River ★★

Swim or snorkel along an 800 m (875 yard) recreation of a tropical river (the water running through here is much warmer than the pools but has no sea life). You will encounter tropical forests along the banks, underwater ruins to explore and the opportunity to swim through a waterfall into the aviary.

If you don't want to take part in any of the swimming activities, or you simply want to rest in the sunshine, you can take your place on one of the numerous sun-beds on the soft white sand and pretend you are at the beach. Relax, and you will think you are a thousand miles away.

EXCURSIONS
Out & about

N

301

50 km
30 miles

ST AUGUSTINE

95

ATLANTIC
OCEAN

Ocala
National
Forest

Lake
George

17

OSCALA

Silver Springs

40

DAYTONA BEACH

19

75

4

ORLANDO

NASA Kennedy
Space Center

SeaWorld

328

Walt Disney
World Resort

COCOA BEACH

KISSIMMEE

Fantasy of Flight

4

Florida's Turnpike

Busch Gardens

CLEARWATER

TAMPA

60

ST PETERSBURG

275

75

27

95

17

Lake
Okeechobee

GULF
OF
MEXICO

75

Busch Gardens
roller coaster excitement

Advertised as 'a wild world', Busch Gardens is to the land what SeaWorld is to the oceans. However, this park is not only a place to see animals from all over the world, it is also a place to enjoy the most exhilarating coasters in Florida. The combination of zoo, wildlife park and fairground makes it one of the most entertaining places to take a family. It is divided into a number of separate areas, themed on exotic African locations.

THINGS TO SEE & DO

Bird Gardens ★★★
The quietest part of the park ,with bird exhibits and shows.

Gwazi ★★★
This dual roller coaster has one lion-coaster and one tiger-coaster that pass within feet of each other six times over the course of the 2134 m (7000 ft) long ride. It recreates the feel of a classic wooden roller coaster as it shakes you around in your seat.

The Land Of The Dragons ★★
A lovely area geared to younger kids under 142 cm (56 inches), with a three-storey tree-house, dragons strolling the paths and a selection of kids' shows.

Congo ★★
A great area for exhilarating rides. **Kumba,** one of the largest roller coasters in the southern USA, reaches 95 km/h (60 mph) and has a loop that plummets 33.5 m (110 ft) and a 360° spiral that leaves you weightless. **Python** whips along like a fast-moving snake and reaches 80 km/h (50 mph). **Congo River Rapids** carries your rubber raft over some realistic white water – be warned, you will get drenched. **Claw Island,** the tiger enclosure, sits in a gorge surrounded by a lagoon. You can look down on the animals lazing or playing in the water below. On **Skyride** you can glide serenely across the park in a four-person aerial gondola, with a view over

the Rhino Rally ride. **Lory Landing** is chock-a-block with colourful parrots, hornbills and pheasants flying free within an enormous, domed aviary.

Edge of Africa ★★★

A walk-through tour of a section of the Serengeti Plain, where plexi-glass screens are all that keep you and the animals apart. You will find a range of African species here including meerkats, vultures, hyenas, lions, crocodiles and baboons, not to mention hippos that you can view from above and below the water. **The KaTonga Musical** is a lavishly produced 35-minute musical featuring African folklore set to song and dance.

Egypt ★★★

Montu, one of the largest inverted roller coasters in the world, reaches a G-force of 3.85, with speeds up to 95 km/h (60 mph) that see you hopping under and over the Busch Gardens railway and high above the plains. Three minutes of total exhilaration. **Tut's Tomb** is a recreation of the treasure rooms found by Howard Carter in the Valley of the Kings in 1922.

Morocco ★★

The entrance area is styled on an oriental Kasbah. Marrakesh Theater hosts **Moroccan Roll**, featuring pop songs with a northern African theme. Watch out for the **Mystic Shieks of Morocco**, an all brass marching band which inspires dance parties through the streets.

Nairobi ★★★

Some heavyweight animal exhibits including elephants, gorillas and chimps. The primate's home is a specially created African central highland environment, one of the largest outside the continent.

Rhino Rally ★★★

This is probably the best single ride in northern Florida for its clever combination of wildlife spotting, well-executed watery surprises and the attention to detail in the landscaping. Rhino Rally takes you on a jeep safari through rhino country (real rhinos too!), where the animals

 *See the wildlife on a jeep safari with a few surprises on the way!*

wander in their park enclosure. Of course, your rally will not go totally to plan – that is the most exciting part! Try to do this ride early or late in the day because the animals seek shade in the heat of the afternoon.

THEME PARK DETAILS
ⓐ Busch Blvd, Tampa ❶ General information 813 987 5082 or 888 800 5447 (freephone in US); Orlando recorded info 407 351 3931 Ⓦ www.buschgardens.com Ⓛ Open high season Mon–Fri 10.00–18.00, weekends 09.00–21.00 ❶ Admission charge

Serengeti Plain ★★★

Similar to Disney's Animal Kingdom Theme Park, the animals (gazelles, giraffe, zebra, rhino and buffalo) roam freely across the 20 ha (50 acre) recreation of an African savannah. The Busch Gardens railway carries you around the area at a sedate speed, giving you plenty of time to view

🔺 *Congo River Rapids at Busch Gardens*

the animals. Alternatively, book your own safari experience, where you head into the heart of the Serengeti Plain in a truck, at Edge of Africa (extra charge).

Stanleyville ★★★

ShiekRa, Busch Gardens' newest roller coaster, is Florida's tallest, and billed as North America's first 'dive coaster'. It's a three-minute, 113 km/h (70 mph) rocket-ride up 61 m (200 ft), then 90° straight down, through an Immelman loop (try to scratch your nose!), then *second* 90° drop... down through a tunnel... and more! **Tanganyika Tidal Wave** takes you through the uncharted waterways of Africa before plummeting over the edge of undiscovered waterfalls. **Stanley Falls** is a roller coaster style log flume ride. The major animal exhibit of Stanleyville is **Orang-utans**. Watch these genetically close cousins at play on their rope swings or rolling about in the hay. **Stanleyville Theater** is home to the 'Jungle Fantasy' stage show featuring acrobatics and circus-style acts.

Timbuktu ★★★

Timbuktu features a range of old-fashioned fairground arcade games and smaller fairground rides for kids. The **Scorpion** roller coaster will provide you with a 360° loop and two minutes of heart-stopping fun.

RESTAURANT

 The Zagora Café $$ There is a large outdoor eating area where you will be serenaded by a Louisiana-style marching brass band.

The Busch Gardens Shuttle Express departs Orlando daily from the Universal bus park at 08.30, SeaWorld bus parking at 08.45, Old Town Shopping Village Kissimmee at 09.15 (except Sat) and Orlando Premium Outlets at 09.30. Tickets are $10 round trip per person or free with a flex-ticket. For reservations (which are required) call ☏ 800 221 1339 (freephone in the US)

Beach resorts
change of pace

CLEARWATER

Head west of Tampa after your visit to Busch Gardens and you will hit the west coast of Florida, which is bounded by the Gulf of Mexico that eventually stretches around to Texas and into Mexico itself. Although there are excellent beaches all along the 'Gulf Coast', as it is known here, **Clearwater** has extra acres of soft white sand and has captured the market as far as hotels and restaurants are concerned. There are no major attractions in the area but the atmosphere is very family orientated, the perfect antidote if you have had too much of Orlando.

COCOA BEACH

The closest beach resort to Orlando is **Cocoa Beach** – a laid back family resort with a long, wide beach and a rustic wooden pier. You can buy bait for fishing or simply sit and have an al fresco lunch, walk for miles along the shore or play volleyball. It is a good place to chill out. One thing that most locals head to Cocoa for is the surfing (though by world standards the waves are not great) and it is the cool place for American college students at spring break.

> ### SHOPPING
> Even if you do not surf, visit **Ron Jon's Surf Shop**, a Florida institution visited by more than 2.4 million people annually. You will be able to buy just about any surf gear, swimwear or tropical clothing here. It is hard to miss this huge pink castle-like building on the main road in town. ⓐ 4151 North Atlantic Ave, Cocoa Beach ⓣ 321 799 8888 ⓦ www.ronjons.com
> ⓛ Open 24 hours

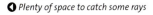
◐ Plenty of space to catch some rays

DAYTONA BEACH

Yet another Florida beach resort, but this is one with a difference. Since the early 1920s, Daytona's name has been synonymous with motor racing. In the early days, lots of speed records were broken here but eventually it was deemed too dangerous to race on the wide, flat, hard-packed sandy beach, though a legacy of that time is that motor vehicles are still allowed out on the sand. Cruising along the beach here at a stately 8 km/h (5 mph) is one of the classic must-do American activities.

Speed fans can still get a thrill at the **Daytona Race Circuit** opened in 1959, where both bike and car formulas meet throughout the year (For dates and ticket details ☎ 904 253 7223). Next door to the circuit is **Daytona USA**, where you can test your skills at changing a wheel in a pit stop, take a guided tour of the track or try three laps in the hands of a professional driver (🅰 1801 W. International Speed Blvd ☎ 386 947 6800 🌐 www.daytonausa.com). **The Richard Petty Driving Experience** also offers an extensive range of driving experiences (☎ 800 237 3889 🌐 www.1800bepetty.com 🕐 Open 09.00–19.00 except Christmas)

🔺 *Daytona beach has a long legacy of motor racing*

Fantasy of Flight
flying high

The largest private collection of rare and vintage aircraft in the world, Fantasy of Flight is the personal dream come true of multi-millionaire Kermit Weeks and it is still expanding. It's a fascinating place to explore, especially for lovers of aircraft.

Whet your appetite with the film **History of Flight** before heading for the **Vintage Aircraft** hangers with over 40 specimens, including the Spitfire of World War II fame. At **Fightertown** you can try your hand in a World War II fighter simulator to take on the enemy in aerial combat. ⓐ 1400 Broadway Blvd, Polk City ⓘ 863 984 3500 ⓦ www.fantasyofflight.com ⓒ Open daily 09.00–17.00 ⓘ Admission charge

⤢ Aviation buffs should take one of the guided tours to view works in progress, and bi-plane, warbird and balloon rides are highly recommended.

⬥ *Be amazed at the world's largest collection of vintage planes*

NASA Kennedy Space Center
to boldly go...

When the space race reached its climax in the late 1960s, the eyes of the whole world were on the Kennedy Space Center on the east coast of Florida, about 45 minutes from Orlando. This was the nerve centre of operations, a place where the then state-of-the-art technology allowed humans to land on the moon and to return safely back to earth. Now it is home to the Space Shuttle programme and one of the earth's two working spaceports – and the only one open to the public. There is really nothing quite as thrilling as watching a shuttle rising from its launch pad. If there is a launch during your stay, try not to miss it.

THINGS TO SEE & DO

A visit has two main components: exhibits at the Visitor Complex and the Kennedy Space Center coach tour.

 If you arrive at the Space Center around late morning, take the tour first when most American visitors will be thinking about lunch.

VISITOR COMPLEX

Your visit will start at the Visitor Complex, the exhibition area for the Kennedy complex which has a range of exhibits and activities.

Astronaut Encounter ★★★

Chat to a real astronaut and find out what food tastes like in space.

Early Space Exploration ★★

This exhibit takes you back to the build up to orbit. Pride of place is taken by a reconstruction of the control centre for the early Mercury space launches and it is amazing to think that today's home PC has more computing power than they had at their fingertips.

● *The Rocket Garden, Kennedy Space Center*

CENTER DETAILS
🅰 On the SR 405 east (NASA Parkway) ℹ 321 449 4444
🅦 www.kennedyspacecenter.com 🕐 Open 09.00–17.30 or later
(except Christmas and launch days) ❗ Admission charge

Exploration in the New Millennium ★★
Lots of fun hands-on scientific stuff for children. The highlight is being able to touch a piece of rock that was brought back from Mars.

Mad Mission to Mars Show ★★
This is the kind of science class that you wanted at school with lots of kooky experiments and audience participation.

Robot Scouts ★★
A display explaining the role of unmanned space flights such as probes bringing back information from the surrounding planets.

Rocket Garden ★
Your chance to get close to some of the old rockets that provided the thrust to break out of the earth's atmosphere.

Shuttle Plaza ★★★
Look inside a full-sized replica of the Space Shuttle to see how little room the astronauts live in while on their missions. Head across the square to Launch Status Center to hear flight briefings every hour and get an overview of the launch programme.

THE SPACE CENTER COACH TOUR
The visitor complex exhibits are excellent, but they should be taken as a whole with the coach tour, which takes you behind the scenes into the real working part of the Space Center. The bus makes three stops, but there's a lot to observe as you travel between them.

Apollo/Saturn V Center ★★★

This stop brings the space race and the first landing on the moon back to life. You can examine a full-scale recreation of the Apollo control centre and relive the tension by watching actual footage of the missions.

The LC-39 Observation Gantry ★★★

From the top of LC-39 you'll get some of the best panoramic views in Florida. You'll easily spot the huge Space Shuttle launch pads and the Vehicle Assembly Building (VAB) whose interior is so large it has rained inside. There is also a theatre presentation and interactive exhibit room.

The Astronaut Hall of Fame ★★

This fascinating attraction has personal insights from the astronauts themselves, highlighting their role from the first manned missions through to the Space Shuttle and Space Station programmes. Kids will enjoy the interactive elements in **Astronaut Adventure** with its G-Force machines and flight simulators. ➌ On the SR 405 east (NASA Parkway) ➊ 321 269 6100 Ⓦ www.astronauthalloffame.com Ⓛ Open 10.00–18.30 ➊ Admission charge

SHUTTLE LAUNCHES

To find out if there are any launches scheduled during your holiday, contact Kennedy Space Center (➊ 321 449 4400) or look on the website (Ⓦ www.kennedyspacecenter.com). For free tickets to the special viewing area, phone (➊ 321 449 4400) or apply online (Ⓦ www.ksctickets.com/kennedyspacecenter). You may also write at least three months in advance (ⓐ NASA Visitor Services, Mail Code: PA-PASS, Kennedy Space Center Visitor Center, FL 32899). If you are not lucky enough to get a ticket, stake out a spot along Highway 1 or A1A (especially the inter-coastal sections), where you can still get a great view. As a last resort, you can see the shuttle from much of the state soon after blast off, just look up.

Silver Springs
crystal-clear waters

Based around one of the largest freshwater springs in the world, Silver Springs is a 142 ha (350 acre) park with a focus on nature. The stunningly clear waters emanating through the rock form the source of the Silver River, and the balance of beautiful gardens, untamed river banks, boat rides and some excellent animal exhibits make for a pleasant day.

THINGS TO SEE & DO
Big Gator Lagoon ★★★
This attraction really lives up to its name, with lots of huge denizens lying in 0.4 ha (1 acre) of genuine cypress swampland – their natural habitat.

Birds of Prey ★★
A show that highlights the tremendous strength, flexibility and accuracy of the large bird species.

Botanical Gardens ★★★
Do take time to stroll through the botanical gardens, with more than 130 varieties of native and exotic plants, floral sculptures and flower beds.

Crocodile Encounter ★★★
Crocs from around the world are here, from the Australian 'salty' to the rapier-snouted fish-eating gharial. ● Feeding 14.30 daily in summer

Florida Natives ★★
A collection of animals still found in the backwoods of the state, including several species of snakes, otters and turtles.

The Fort King River Cruise ★★★
Glide and walk through Silver Springs' 10,000 year history and you'll visit an actual archaeological dig site, a reconstructed Seminole Indian village and a 19th-century Fort King Army stockade.

▲ *Glass-bottom boat, Silver Springs*

Glass-bottom boat trips ★ ★ ★

These carry you along the upper reaches of the Silver River and around the springhead itself, revealing a wealth of wildlife including turtles, huge freshwater fish, herons, egrets, waterfowl and the occasional baby 'gator.

Kritter Korral ★ ★

This is a petting-zoo for the little ones, with soft, friendly farm animals

Lost River Voyage ★ ★ ★

Explore an untamed stretch of the river and its dense forest canopy for native wildlife spotting. Includes a trip to the park's veterinary hospital.

Panther Prowl ★ ★ ★

This attraction has two aims, to breed panthers in captivity, and to educate visitors about this beautiful species which is in extreme danger of extinction. Only a plexi-glass screen separates human and beast.

Ross Allen Island Animal Shows ★ ★

Three different shows featuring reptiles, birds and creepy-crawlies.

World of Bears ★ ★ ★

The largest captive bear collection in the world covers over 0.8 ha (2 acres) and features grizzlies and brown bears, among others.

THEME PARK DETAILS
🅐 East of Ocala on the SR40 (exit 352 east off I-75 or exit 268 west off I-95) ☎ 352 236 2121 🆆 www.silversprings.com
🕐 Open throughout the year 10.00–17.00 ❶ Admission charge

St Augustine
historical attractions

St Augustine is the oldest continuously occupied settlement in the United States. In 1565, Spanish forces under Pedro Menéndez de Avilés founded the town, which then changed nationality several times between the Spanish and the English before American independence. Many of St Augustine's historic buildings still remain, and the old downtown area recreates life in those early days so you can really get a feel for the founding of this new country.

THINGS TO SEE & DO

Castillo San Marco ★ ★ ★

Built by the Spanish, the fort town was finished in 1697 and is one of only a handful in North America. You can walk around the battlements and take in the panoramic views. During the summer, battles are re-enacted on the pristine lawns within the castle grounds – it is thrilling stuff with the clash of iron and the smell of gunpowder. ⓐ 1 Castillo Dr., off Avenida Menéndez ⓣ 904 829 6506 ⓛ Open 08.45–16.45 ⓘ Admission charge, check with the tourist board for exact dates

Historic St Augustine ★ ★ ★

In the collection of tiny narrow streets at the heart of the modern town you are transported back in time to 18th-century St Augustine. The Gonzáles-Alvarez House claims to be the oldest in the town and is open as a museum. Head to traffic-free St George Street where you will find residents dressed in Spanish costumes waiting to give you the low-down on life as a settler in the 1600s, and you can watch artisans at work in the Spanish Quarter. ⓐ St George Street ⓛ All historic St Augustine museums and attractions open 09.00–17.00 ⓘ Admission charge for Gonzáles-Alvarez House and the Spanish Quarter

◗ *Castillo San Marco*

The Lightner Museum ★

This intriguing museum decorated with Tiffany glass houses the vast collections of 'objets d'art' accumulated by newspaper magnate Otto C Lightner. ⓐ 75 King St ⓣ 904 824 2874 ⓛ Open 09.00–17.00 ⓘ Admission charge

St Augustine Sightseeing Trains ★★

Let the train take the strain on this hour-long journey, as you travel past the important historic monuments. ⓣ 904 829 6545 or 800 226 6545 (freephone in the US)

St Petersburg
cultural centre

Sitting on the south-western coast of Tampa Bay, St Petersburg is a sophisticated coastal city that is not reliant upon tourism for its living. Quite a contrast to both Orlando and St Augustine in atmosphere, being busy with commerce and daily life, St Petersburg has world-class art museums and an interesting history.

THINGS TO SEE & DO
Museum of Fine Arts ★★★
A surprisingly rich collection of European, American, Greek and Roman as well as renowned pre-Columbian and Asian art is supplemented by touring exhibits from around the world. ⓐ 255 Beach Drive NE, near **The Pier** ⓣ 727 896 2667 ⓦ www.fine-arts.org ⓛ Open Tues–Sat 10.00–17.00, Sun 13.00–17.00, closed Mon ⓘ Admission charge

The Pier ★★
Tourists flock to this long pier, jutting into Tampa Bay, for the shopping (there's a five-storey mall at the eastern end), fishing (rent gear) and pelican feeding. Worth a stroll. ⓐ 800 2nd Ave NE ⓣ 727 647 1538 ⓛ Open Mon–Thurs 10.00–21.00, Fri–Sat 10.00–22.00, Sun 11.00–19.00

Salvador Dali Museum ★★★
One of the world's largest collections of the Spanish surrealist's paintings. ⓐ 1000 3rd Street South ⓣ 727 823 3767 or 800 442 3254 (freephone in US) ⓦ www.salvadordalimuseum.org ⓛ Open Mon–Wed and Sat 09.30–17.30, Thurs 09.30–20.00, Sun noon–17.30 ⓘ Admission charge

St Petersburg Historical and Flight One Museum ★
The world's first scheduled passenger flight took place from St Petersburg's lovely airport. This small museum commemorates that event. ⓐ 335 North Second Ave ⓣ 727 894 1052 ⓛ Open Mon noon–19.00, Tues–Sat 10.00–17.00, Sun noon–17.00 ⓘ Admission charge

Food & drink

Eating is one of the great pleasures of a trip to Orlando. It is difficult to walk more than a few yards without passing an opportunity to snack on finger food, grab some fast food, or indulge in a full meal with table service.

WHEN TO EAT

You can take breakfast from around 07.00 and this can be anything from continental style (often provided at hotels), to vast 'eat all you want' buffets of hot and cold dishes served at family restaurants. This can keep you going until dinner. Americans love to 'brunch' and you can eat as late as 11.00.

Lunch is served in the middle of the day and many restaurants that are more formal will have set hours (11.00–15.00).

Americans generally eat dinner early and restaurants are often at their busiest between 18.00–19.30. Don't worry if you want to eat later, most places stay open until 22.00 and later at weekends.

● *You can't leave Orlando without sampling a burger*

PROTOCOL

Most restaurants will ask you to wait to be seated. This is so that each of the waiting staff has a balanced workload. You may have the choice of a smoking or non-smoking table, although many restaurants no longer have smoking areas. If you want a particular table ask for it – your request will normally be granted. And don't forget to tip! Fifteen per cent of the bill is normal.

FAST FOOD & SNACKS

America was the birthplace of the fast-food revolution, so it is not surprising that you will find as many snack joints as formal restaurants. You can eat on the move or sit at dinette seats. Choose from burgers, pizza, sandwiches, bagels, ice cream, churros (sweet fried fritters) or popcorn.

Family-oriented restaurants will often have a 'one child eats free with each adult' policy, and 'early bird' specials also save money (eat dinner before 18.00). Several booklets offer discounts to many of the well-known chains of restaurants.

WHAT TO EAT

There is no end of choice as far as 'good ole' American cuisine is concerned. Steaks come in all shapes and sizes, from junior to Homer Simpson size. Barbequed chicken and ribs are another juicy alternative.

Orlando is not far from the sea in any direction and seafood is abundant, fresh and delicious. Local fish, including grouper, dolphin fish (not the loveable sea mammal, but a large fish also called Mahi Mahi or Dorado) and wahoo, form the basis of many dishes; or try the snow crabs, shrimps or fresh imported lobster.

Many restaurants allow you to order 'combo' meals. This means a meat/chicken/seafood combination or mixture of other ingredients.

The cultural mix of Florida means that the world is available on a plate. There is a choice of Caribbean-style spicy foods, Chinese and Thai dishes, Cuban, Mexican and familiar old Italian recipes. You certainly do not have to eat the same type of food twice during your holiday. You will not find over-spicy food here, as Americans generally do not like food too hot or 'garlicky'.

It is difficult to just order a simple item – salads come with numerous dressings; coffee comes decaf, with milk, cream, chocolate or nuts; and be specific about what kind of cola you want – regular, diet or caffeine-free.

DRINKS

You will be offered plain iced water with your meal always – great for rehydrating but not very exciting. Coffee and tea are available everywhere, hot or iced, and many family restaurants will give you as many free refills as you can take.

Soda (pop) is the drink of choice for most Americans, with Coke and Pepsi the main cola brand names. Florida is famous for its fresh orange juice and you can order this at most establishments. Smoothies are widely available and are very refreshing on a hot day.

ALCOHOL

American beer is of the light lager variety, served cold. It is cheapest on draught, as in the UK, but you can get it in bottles. Smaller breweries make darker, more fully flavoured beers so do ask your server for advice if you want something with a little more bite.

Wine is readily available and mostly Californian, bold cabernets, white and red zinfandels and fruity merlot, though Australian, Chilean and French wines are easy to locate as well. Americans sometimes call rosé wine, 'blush'.

Cocktails are inexpensive and popular, and many bars have daily specials or house cocktails with exotic names. Frozen cocktails are a little like smoothies, but with a shot or two of alcohol so definitely not for kids.

Remember: the legal age to consume alcohol is 21. Bars are strict and staff may ask for photographic ID – carry your passport as proof of age, even if you are well above the legal age. Drink driving rules are strictly enforced, and one beer, wine or cocktail puts you at the legal limit.

Menu decoder

GENERAL

place setting/silverware
   cutlery
broiled grilled
grilled flame grilled
appetiser starter
entrée main course

BREAKFAST

eggs 'over easy' eggs fried
   both sides but still soft
eggs 'sunny side up'
   eggs fried only on one side
biscuit savoury scone
hash browns grated potato, fried
grits ground boiled corn, like savoury porridge but stiffer
jelly jam

Florida is famous for its orange juice

OTHER FOOD THAT MAY CONFUSE YOU

french fries chips

chips crisps

cookie biscuit

shrimp prawn

conch (pronounced 'conk') marine sea snail (more delicious than you can imagine)

chowder a thick soup

liquor spirits (gin, whisky etc)

shot measure

Portions are gargantuan by British standards. Consider splitting the main course with a friend or spouse, even if a small fee applies. And don't be shy to ask for any leftover food to be packed up for you to take with you if you want to eat it later (in a 'doggie bag'); it is a common practice.

Shopping

Retail therapy is one of the major attractions of a trip to Orlando. Americans know how to make shopping fun and easy with shops being open from 10.00 until at least 21.00 every day except Sunday. Credit cards are universally accepted and with prices of many goods being dollars for pounds, savings are at least 30 per cent on prices in the UK.

Remember your luggage weight allowance for the flight home. Most charter companies are very strict about this and you may have to pay excess ($10 per kg at present) on anything over 20 kg (44 lb) per person (15 kg/33 lb per person if you booked a last-minute package).

WHAT TO BUY

Branded goods are the must-buy items. Clothing is the most popular, and in a way it would make sense to travel light and buy everything when you arrive from all the top American high-street brands including Banana Republic, Timberland, Tommy Hilfiger, Gap and Levi's.

There is an abundance of sportswear by all the big names, from trainers to shorts and shirts. Many styles will not have been seen back home yet.

Clothing sizes are one size smaller than in the UK – if you are a size 10, you should ask for a size 8 in the US. Shoes sizes are one or two sizes bigger – if you are a size 5 in the UK, you are a size 6 in the US, and a size 8 in the UK is a size 10 in the US.

Be aware that videos may not play on your machine back home. DVDs certainly won't unless you have a Region 1 or region-free player. Electrical goods run on 110 volts in the US and so will not work in the UK without a transformer, however note that most notebook computers come with transformers which run on power from 100V (Japanese standard) to 240V; all you need to do on return is change the lead to have a British plug. Don't forget to add 6 per cent to all ticket prices. This is Florida state tax and will be added on at the till.

WHERE TO SHOP

America invented the shopping mall and Orlando has its fair share. A plus for the city is that most of the malls close to the main tourist areas are outlet malls, with substantial savings even on normal American prices. These goods can be line ends or slight seconds.

Prime Outlets Orlando is at the heart of the action at the northern tip of I-Drive. The largest outlet mall in the area, it has more than 170 stores with well-known brand names such as Levi's, Reebok, Calvin Klein and Tommy Hilfiger (see page 23).

Exercise your credit card

Florida Outlet Mall in Lake Buena Vista is more upmarket with names such as Giorgio Armani and MaxMara.

Normal malls still offer good value and perhaps a better range of goods. The nearest to the tourist centres is **Florida Mall** on Sand Lake Drive intersection with Orange Blossom Trail, out to the east (☎ 407 851 6255).

I-Drive has its own stores, often selling basic souvenirs featuring Disney characters cheaper than at the attractions themselves, although the quality is not always as good. **Pointe Orlando** is where you can find more well-known brand names (see page 23).

You can be sure that the exit of many attractions and theme parks will lead right through the large shops. Some of the best are at Disney and Universal as you would expect, but there are also good shops at Jungleland, Gatorland and Busch Gardens. Downtown Disney and CityWalk at Universal Studios both have shops in a fun, mall style – you do not even have to enter the parks to get your branded souvenirs.

Most of the major theme parks will deliver your purchases to a collection point near the exit, so that you can collect them as you leave.

Kids

Orlando is kid heaven. Where else could you spend up to two weeks in a total fantasy world, get up close with dolphins, play all day on water slides or stare into the jaws of an alligator? It is not just the attractions either. Because children form a large percentage of Orlando's visitors, they are made to feel at home right across the resort.

EVENING SHOWS

Where most resorts might pack the kids off to bed early, Orlando offers them a wealth of exciting evening shows where they can cheer the 'goodies' and boo the 'baddies'. Best for small children is **Pirate's Dinner Adventure** (see page 20) – almost like a pantomime with plenty of opportunities for the kids to get involved. Older children will love the horse show at **Arabian Nights** (see page 30) while teenagers might go for **Medieval Times** (see page 31) with lots of knights and swordfights.

THEME PARKS

If you have very young children, **Magic Kingdom Park** is where you can spend a lot of time. If you have teenagers, head for **Universal Studios** or **Epcot**. In general, the other parks, from **Islands of Adventure** to **Disney's Animal Kingdom Theme Park** and **Disney-MGM Studios**, have a very broad appeal for all age groups, as do **SeaWorld** and **Busch Gardens**. **Silver Springs** has very good animal exhibits but no roller coasters.

WATER PARKS

This is a good way to cool down and have fun. **Wet 'n Wild** (see page 17) is an excellent park, and Disney has several for you to choose from.

 Rent a pushchair (stroller) at all the major parks because you will probably find that even the most active child will become tired after a few hours in a theme park.

Sports & activities

AIRBOAT RIDES

Ride out over the swamplands to see how Florida looked fewer than 30 years ago with **Boggy Creek Airboat Rides**. The airboats' big turbine engine is out of the water so they can travel fast across the shallow marshes and rivers around East Lake Tohopekaliga. See alligators, turtles and a range of bird life in its natural habitat.

Boggy Creek also operate night-time alligator viewing trips with advance booking, and parasailing on the freshwater lake beyond a 'gator's range (you don't get wet unless you want to). ⓐ Boggy Creek Rd (Orlando Airport area) ⓘ 407 344 9550 ⓦ www.bcairboats.com ⓛ Open daily 09.00–17.30, rides every 45 minutes

BALLOON RIDES

One of the best ways to get a panoramic view over Orlando and the surrounding area is from a balloon – a silent floating platform that can climb up to 305 m (1000 ft). The conditions are best in the early morning because there is little or no wind and you will meet for your briefing before dawn. There is a very informal atmosphere – the location for launch is decided, depending on local weather conditions, and you race off to get the balloon ready. Flights last around an hour, after which you are welcomed into the ballooning fraternity with a glass of champagne before enjoying a buffet breakfast. **Orange Blossom Balloons** ⓘ 407 239 7677 ⓛ Flights daily ⓘ Admission fee and hotel transfers for a small extra fee

⬥ *Splash around and cool down*

GOLF

With almost 200 golf courses and a near-perfect climate, it's no wonder that many holiday-makers choose to take to the tee in central Florida. Some of the higher-class hotels have been quick to add courses and even Disney has realised there is a market for adults on the greens when the kids are at the theme parks.

The officially endorsed PGA Guide to Golf produces a complimentary magazine full of information and details of public golf courses in Orlando. This is distributed at tourist information centres across the Orlando/Daytona area or get further information at (Ⓦ www.pgatour.com).

Festivals & events

It seems that Orlando is like one long festival and that it would be almost impossible for special events to be given any more razzmatazz. However, theme park 'imagineers' (show, parade and set designers) pull out all the stops with extra special activities added to the already full programmes for major American holidays. The main three are Independence Day (4 July), Thanksgiving (fourth Thursday in November) and Christmas. Americans call late December 'the holidays' because the period covers a time of celebration for other faiths as well as Christians. Disney parades become a riot of even more twinkling lights and Santa Claus spends time finding out just what every little girl or boy wants.

The east coast of Florida has a number of seasonal events. Spring Break is the traditional time when students leave their books and head for the coast, and Cocoa Beach and Daytona are popular destinations. Events include volleyball, surfing and 'chilling out'.

Daytona holds racing events throughout the year, but the major meets are the Daytona 500 and the Daytona 200, usually held in March. Race fans make up a proportion of the visitors, but these events also attract bikers from around America to what are called 'festival' weeks or 'fests' and thousands roll in on their huge Harleys. There is also another 'fest' in late October or early November.

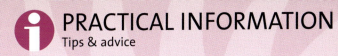

Preparing to go

GETTING THERE

The cheapest way to get to Orlando is to book a package holiday with one of the leading tour operators specialising in US holidays. You should also check the travel supplements of the weekend newspapers, such as *The Sunday Telegraph* and *The Sunday Times*. They often carry adverts for inexpensive flights, as well as classified adverts for privately-owned villas and apartments to rent in most popular holiday destinations. If your travelling times are flexible, and if you can avoid the school holidays, you can also find some very cheap last-minute deals using the websites for the leading holiday companies.

BEFORE YOU LEAVE

Holidays should be about fun and relaxation, so avoid last minute panics and stress by making your preparations well in advance.

It is not necessary to have inoculations to travel in the US, but you should make sure you and your family are up to date with the basics, such as tetanus. It is a good idea to pack a small first-aid kit to carry with you containing plasters (should you need to buy some, note that Americans call these Band Aids and don't understand 'plaster'), antiseptic cream, travel sickness pills, insect repellent and/or bite relief cream, antihistamine tablets, upset stomach remedies and painkillers. If you are taking prescription medicines, ensure that you take enough for the duration of your visit. It is also worth having a dental check-up before you go.

DOCUMENTS

The most important documents you will need are your tickets and your passport. Check well in advance that your passport is up to date and has at least three months left to run (six months is even better). All children, including newborn babies, need their own passport now, unless they are already included on the passport of the person they are travelling with. It generally takes at least three weeks to process a passport renewal. This can be longer in the run-up to the summer months. For the latest information on how to renew your passport and the processing times call the Passport Agency (☏ 0870 521 0410), or access their website (ⓦ www.ukpa.gov.uk).

For UK citizens there is a visa waiver agreement granting you 90 days non-employment stay in the US – you will get a form to fill in on the plane, which you must hand to the immigration official on arrival. Other nationalities may require a visa to enter the US. You should check the details of your travel tickets well before your departure, ensuring that the timings and dates are correct.

If you are thinking of hiring a car while you are away, you will need to have your UK driving licence with you. If you want more than one driver for the car, the other drivers must have their licence too. British disabled driver notices are respected in Florida, so bring yours with you and take advantage of the excellent disabled parking facilities.

MONEY

You will need some currency before you go, especially if your flight gets you to your destination after the banks have closed. Travellers' cheques are the safest way to carry money because the money will be refunded if the cheques are lost or stolen. To buy travellers' cheques or foreign currency at a bank you may need to give up to a week's notice. You can exchange money at the airport before you depart. ATMs or cash dispensers are abundant, and may offer you the best exchange rates. You should make sure that your credit, charge and debit cards are up to date – you do not want them to expire mid holiday – and that your credit limit is sufficient to allow you to make those holiday purchases. Don't forget, too, to check your PIN numbers in case you haven't used them for a while – in order to draw money from cash dispensers while you are away. Ring your bank or card company and they will help you out.

INSURANCE

It's crucial to have a comprehensive medical insurance package when you take a holiday in the United States. If you need medical treatment you will be expected to pay for it and bills can add up even for the simplest ailments or injuries. A visit to a US doctor will start at $100;

a hospital emergency room starts at $350 and can easily run to the thousands or tens of thousands. It's also important to be covered in case you cause injury to others or damage to property because Americans sue far more readily than people in the UK. Look for a package that covers you for medical and personal liability of at least $2,000,000.

You should also insure the things you take with you on holiday, although most policies will have upper limits for items like cameras and jewellery. Delay and cancellation policies will cover you for airport and technical problems, and will refund the money you paid for your holiday if you have to cancel at the last minute – if you're ill, for example. Always check the small print to compare different policies.

CLIMATE

Florida has a tropical climate. If you travel between October and May, expect showers (some heavy) and occasional chilly spells, though the temperature rarely drops below 15°C (60°F) and will reach 27–28°C (the low 80°Fs) during the day. In summer you may still encounter afternoon downpours, but the temperatures are generally around 30–32°C (the high 80°Fs) and the nights are warm. Hurricane season is from June to November. While these storms are well-predicted and generally only a minor inconvenience to holiday-makers, hurricanes are deadly, and warnings should be heeded.

Orlando is a casual destination and shorts, T-shirts and sandals are great for most daytime and evening activities. Holiday-makers enjoy dressing for dinner but it's not generally necessary and it is more the exception for restaurants to require men to wear a jacket and tie. Swimwear is not acceptable beyond the confines of the pool area. Take a sweater in winter in case of a cold spell.

At all times of year the atmosphere can be very humid as the rain evaporates. The sun will be very hot so take plenty of sun protection, a hat and sun glasses for each member of the family. One vital point is footwear. You'll probably be walking an awfully long way around the theme parks so take something comfortable. This is not the place to break in new holiday shoes.

SECURITY

Take sensible precautions to prevent your house being burgled while you are away:

- Cancel milk, newspapers and other regular deliveries so that post and milk does not pile up on the doorstep, indicating that you are away.
- Let the postman know where to leave parcels and bulky mail that will not go through your letterbox – ideally with a next-door neighbour.
- If possible, arrange for a friend or neighbour to visit regularly, closing and opening curtains in the evening and morning, and switching lights on and off to give the impression that the house is being lived in.
- Consider buying electrical timing devices that will switch lights and radios on and off, again to give the impression you are still at home.
- Let Neighbourhood Watch representatives know that you will be away so that they can keep an eye on your home.
- If you have a burglar alarm, make sure that it is serviced and working properly and is switched on when you leave (you may find that your insurance policy requires this). Ensure that a neighbour is able to gain access to the alarm to turn it off if it is set off accidentally.
- If you are leaving cars unattended, put them in a garage, if possible, and leave a key with a neighbour in case the alarm goes off.

AIRPORT PARKING AND ACCOMMODATION

If you intend to leave your car in an airport car park while you are away, or stay the night at an airport hotel before or after your flight, you should book well ahead to take advantage of discounts or cheap off-airport parking. Airport accommodation gets booked up several weeks in advance, especially during the height of the holiday season. Check whether the hotel offers free parking for the duration of the holiday – often the savings made on parking costs can significantly reduce the accommodation price.

PACKING TIPS

Baggage allowances vary according to the airline, destination and the class of travel, but 20 kg (44 lb) per person is the norm for luggage that is carried in the hold (it usually tells you what the weight limit is on your ticket). You are also allowed one item of cabin baggage weighing no more than 5 kg (11 lb), and measuring 46 by 30 by 23cm (18 by 12 by 9 inches).

In addition, you can usually carry your duty-free purchases, umbrella, handbag, coat, camera, etc, as hand baggage. Large items – surfboards, golf-clubs, collapsible wheelchairs and pushchairs – are usually charged as extras and it is a good idea to let the airline know in advance that you want to bring these.

CHECK-IN, PASSPORT CONTROL AND CUSTOMS

First-time travellers can often find airport security intimidating, but it is all very easy really.

- Check-in desks usually open two or three hours before the flight is due to depart. Arrive early for the best choice of seats.
- Look for your flight number on the TV monitors in the check-in area, and find the relevant check-in desk. Your tickets will be checked and your luggage taken. Take your boarding card and go to the departure gate. Here your hand luggage will be X-rayed and your passport checked.
- In the departure area, you can shop and relax, but watch the monitors that tell you when to board – usually about 30 minutes before take-off. Go to the departure gate shown on the monitor and follow the instructions given to you by the airline staff.

During your stay

AIRPORTS

Orlando has two airports. Orlando International is south east of the city and handles scheduled and some holiday charter flights, and Orlando-Sanford Airport is 48 km (30 miles) north east of the city and deals only with holiday flights. Before you enter the United States you'll be asked to complete a customs form and you will not be allowed to take any raw foods into the country. Duty free limits for entry are one litre of spirits or wine (travellers must be over 21), 120 cigarettes or 100 cigars (not Cuban) and up to $100 worth of gifts.

If you are travelling with a tour operator you will be met by a rep outside the arrivals terminal. Fly/drive passengers will find the major car hire companies within the Arrivals terminal at Orlando International and just across the road from the Arrivals terminal in Sanford.

BEACHES

In summer, many beaches have life guards and a flag safety system. Observe beach warning flags and never enter the sea when the yellow or red flags are flying. Other beaches may be safe for swimming but there are unlikely to be life-saving amenities available. Bear in mind that strong winds can quickly change a safe beach into a not-so-safe one, and some can have strong currents further out. If in doubt, ask your local tour representative or at your hotel.

BEACH SAFETY

Most beaches where the public bathe in numbers operate a flag system to indicate the sea conditions.

- **Red or black** = dangerous – no swimming
- **Yellow** = good swimmers only – apply caution
- **Green or white** = safe bathing conditions for all

CHILDREN'S ACTIVITIES

It goes without saying that Orlando is a paradise for children, with no shortage of theme parks and activities to choose from. The climate is probably better in winter for younger children (15–26°C or 60–80°F). Summer can be hot and you'll need to take care of young skin and keep kids hydrated with plenty of drinks.

CONSULATE

British Consul offices:

ⓐ Sunbank Tower, Suite 2110, South Orange Avenue, Orlando FL 32801

ⓣ 407 426 7855

CURRENCY

The currency in the United States is the US dollar ($). Each dollar (commonly called bucks, but also known as greenbacks because of their colour) is made up of 100 cents. Coin denominations are 1 cent (called a penny), 5 cents (nickel), 10 cents (dime) and 25 cents (quarter). Notes (bills) are $1, $5, $10, $20 $50 and $100. All dollar bills are the same size and colour, so be careful when you pay with cash. Always check the amount on the note.

ELECTRICITY

American electrical voltage is 110 volts and electrical items such as hairdryers and shavers you bring from home will be a little slower or less powerful. You'll also need an adapter plug with two flat pins to fit an American electrical socket. If you are buying electrical appliances to take home, always check that they will work in the UK before you buy.

FACILITIES FOR THE VISITORS WITH DISABILITIES

In the US, all businesses that deal with the public, including hotels, attractions and restaurants, are required by law to have facilities for people with disabilities. International Drive has lowered kerbs at all crossing points and intersections to allow for easier road crossing and the theme parks have designated routes for visitors with disabilities. Most shops and restaurants have parking bays for disabled drivers. A British disabled parking badge will be recognized here so if you have one, bring it with you. Individual rides in the theme parks will have differing rules, so enquire with the parks themselves about restrictions.

GETTING AROUND

Car hire Car hire is easy in Orlando and at first glance prices are cheap. However, this basic price doesn't include insurance, taxes and other surcharges. These can more than double the final cost. Don't accept the fuel purchase option – touted as a money saver – unless you're positive you can return the car running on fumes. Choose to return the car with a full tank of gas, then make sure it's actually full before returning it, or pay $5 per gallon for them to fill it for you. Packages bought in the UK will often include all these extras so it's worthwhile shopping around. Make sure that you have Collision Damage Waiver (CDW), also known as Loss Damage Waiver (LDW), which will cover you for any damage to the car whatever the cause. Liability or Extended Protection covers you in case you cause an accident, important in this litigation-crazy country.

Driving Americans drive on the right. Speed limits are signposted on the roadside and alter frequently, so keep your eyes on them.

Traffic is controlled more by traffic lights at intersections than roundabouts. Traffic can turn right at a red light after first coming to a complete stop unless signs say it's forbidden (watch out for people crossing the road before you do).

Road names are hung above the intersection. The name you can read is the road you are crossing, not the road you are on.

Do not overtake yellow school buses when they have their flashing lights on. When they stop so must you, even when you are on the other side of the road.

When on dual carriageways cars can pass on either side and some exits are on the left of the carriageway.

Do not drink and drive: there are serious penalties even for a first-time offender, and one drink of beer, wine or a cocktail will put you at the legal limit.

Always carry your driving licence and car hire papers when you are driving the car. If you are stopped by the police do not get out of the car; put both hands on the steering wheel until advised otherwise by an officer. Note that 'car stops' are the single most dangerous aspect of American police work, so officers (who are all armed) are highly alert when they approach a stopped car. Place both your hands on the steering wheel (and have passengers keep hands visible and still) until advised otherwise by an officer.

If another motorist signals that there is something wrong with your car, or nudges the back of your car, do not stop straight away. Drive to a public place such as a petrol station just in case it is a hoax.

If you have an accident the police must be called before you move your car. Your car hire firm should give you a number to call in case of a breakdown. However, if you are on a major highway, raise the bonnet of your car and a passing police patrol will offer assistance. Dial 911 if it's an emergency.

Pay particular attention to local parking restrictions. Do not park within 3 m (10 ft) of a fire hydrant or lowered kerb. Do not park at the roadside. Most restaurants and shops have ample parking. Park bonnet first so that the registration tag, on the rear, can be seen. Do not park against the direction of traffic, or you will be ticketed.

Driving vocabulary is different from the UK:

USA	UK	USA	UK
gas	petrol	*freeway*	motorway
gas pedal	accelerator	*no standing*	no parking or stopping
trunk	car boot	*ramp*	slip road
hood	car bonnet	*yield*	give way
fender	car bumper	*downtown*	city centre
windshield	windscreen		

Public transport The Lynx bus system operates throughout the Orlando metropolitan area. They can be contacted on phone (☏ 407 841 5969) or on the web (🌐 www.golynx.com). The main routes (or lines) that are helpful to visitors are 56 (Highway 192 in Kissimmee to the Magic Kingdom Park) and 50 (I-Drive to the Magic Kingdom Park). Generally there is one bus every 30 minutes and ticket prices are cheap.

I-Drive has its own trolleybus service called I-Ride running along its 9.5 km (6 mile) length and along Universal Boulevard running parallel to I-Drive to the east. It runs 07.00–23.30 at 15-minute intervals. Prices are cheap but have plenty of coins because the correct fare is needed. Day passes for up to 14 days are available. They can be contacted on phone (☏ 407 248 9590) or on the web (🌐 www.iridetrolley.com).

HEALTH MATTERS

Emergency medical and dental care Facilities for emergency treatment are very good with a number of private hospitals in the area. Dentists are very well qualified but you'll have to pay. You'll probably have to claim the money you pay to a dentist back from your insurance company after you return home. Dial 911 in any emergency.

Chemists Known as pharmacies or drug stores, chemists are well stocked with items for mild health problems and you will probably find the choice of products a little overwhelming. Every area will have a pharmacy that is open 24 hours (Eckerd or Walgreens are the most numerous).

Water You can drink the tap water in Orlando but it can taste different from tap water at home. Bottled water is widely available.

THE LANGUAGE

Although Americans speak English and you should have little difficulty in being understood, there are many differences in vocabulary and sometimes the same word can mean something totally different in the US. Some useful phrases for drivers are listed opposite but here are a few other general words and phrases that might help:

USA	UK	USA	UK
crib	baby cot	elevator	lift
diaper	nappy	fanny pack	bum bag
stroller	pushchair	faucet	tap
line	queue	purse	handbag

MEDIA

Most hotels and motels will have satellite or cable TV service with over 20 channels to choose from. Major news channels include CNN and there is a range of entertainment and specialist channels (shopping, religion, films etc).

There are plenty of radio stations to choose from, each offering a different kind of music, from rock to pop to blues – though the numerous adverts may get on your nerves.

OPENING HOURS

Banks Open Monday–Friday 09.00–15.00, and some on Saturday
09.00–13.00, but there are numerous 24-hour ATM machines where you
can withdraw cash on a Cirrus, NYCE or credit card, and most establishments accept travellers' cheques in payment. Note that foreign currency
exchange is not a standard service in American banks.

Shops In the tourist areas open around 10.00 and stay open until 22.00,
though shops in the non-tourist areas open Monday–Saturday 10.00–21.00
and 11.00–20.00 on Sunday. Pharmacies are open the same time as other
shops but there will always be a 24-hour pharmacy in the area.

Restaurants Opening times vary enormously. Family restaurants can
be open as early as 07.00 serving enormous breakfast buffets and stay
open all day until 22.00. You'll find much the same hours for fast-food
restaurants. More upmarket restaurants will open for lunch 11.00–15.00
and again for dinner 17.00–22.00.

Museums Open daily 09.00–17.00 but the tourist attractions open longer
hours; the theme parks keep visitors happy with shows and parades
from 09.00 until midnight, though times do vary with season.

Christian churches There is a variety of denominations and service times
are always displayed on a board at the entrance.

PERSONAL COMFORT AND SECURITY

Making a complaint The United States prides itself on its service so
don't be afraid to complain if there is something that you are not
satisfied with. Speak to the duty manager and explain simply what
the problem is – they should make every effort to resolve it to your
satisfaction.

Laundry The majority of hotels will offer a laundry facility where your
clothes are sent out to be washed or dry cleaned, but will charge a high
price for each item. Some family resorts have on-site laundries for their
guests – check with your travel agent before booking.

Public toilets The major attractions are well kitted out with toilet facilities
and shopping malls have free facilities – including family facilities. When

WHAT TO DO IN AN EMERGENCY

As in the UK, there is one emergency number for all the emergency services. You will be asked to state which service you want by the operator. The emergency number is **911**.

you want to know where the public toilets are, ask for the 'rest room' or 'bathroom'. It's considered vulgar to ask for the toilet.

Lost property Lost property will normally be kept with the manager of an establishment so if it's a restaurant or shop try going back to ask if something has been handed in. At larger malls or theme parks, guest services will be able to help you.

Valuables, crime and the police Serious crime against tourists is rare but you can minimize your chances of becoming a victim by taking the following precautions.

- Don't carry large amounts of cash, and don't flash cash around when you buy things in shops. Pay with a credit card where possible and keep your card in a safe place.
- Leave all valuables such as plane tickets, extra travellers' cheques and cash in the hotel safe. You may have to pay a small daily charge to use this but the peace of mind is worth it.
- Don't leave bags lying around at cafés and nightspots.
- Take all valuables out of the car whenever you leave it. See section on driving for other security advice.
- Don't open your hotel door to strangers and don't invite people back to your room.
- If you become a victim of crime, don't put up a fight as the criminals may be armed. Dial 911 for the police.
- You will need a police report if you want to claim on your insurance for any missing money or property. If you are given the original of this form, rather than a photocopy, hang on to it and take photocopies to give anyone who requests one.

POST OFFICES

The US Postal Service offers a reliable and speedy service, but there are not many post offices in the tourist areas. If you only want to send post cards home it's much easier to buy stamps from local shops or supermarkets and post them at your hotel. A post-box is called a mailbox in America.

RELIGION

America is a predominantly Christian country with many denominations. Masses and services are held on Sundays (some denominations on Saturdays). Your hotel will have details of the closest churches to you.

TELEPHONES

If you need to call home it will be very expensive to do so through your hotel – they charge as much as 50 per cent excess. Better to buy a fixed-price calling card at a drug store or supermarket (some British holiday company offices also sell them). You then call a special number to route your calls either from your hotel room or from a public phone (look for signs of a white telephone handset on a blue background).

TIME DIFFERENCES

Orlando is five hours behind the time at home, on US Eastern Standard Time (EST) in winter, and US Eastern Daylight Time (EDT) in summer. This means that if it's noon in the UK, it's 07.00 in Orlando.

TIPPING

As a basic guide leave 15 per cent at restaurants, offer the same to taxi drivers, and give your room cleaner $1 per day for each room occupant.

INTERNATIONAL DIALLING CODES

To call the US from the UK, dial 00 1 then the nine-digit number – there's no need to wait for a dialling tone. For calls to the UK, dial 011 44, then take off the first 0 of the UK code before dialling.

ACKNOWLEDGEMENTS

We would like to thank all the photographers, picture libraries and organisations for the loan of the photographs reproduced in this book, to whom copyright in the photograph belongs:
© Disney (pages 40, 43, 44, 45, 48-49, 51, 55, 57);
Andre Jenny/Alamy (page 91);
Jupiter Images Corporation (pages 111, 125);
Pete Bennett (All others).

We would also like to thank the following for their contribution to this series:
John Woodcock (map and symbols artwork);
Katie Greenwood (picture research);
Patricia Baker, Rachel Carter, Judith Chamberlain-Webber, Nicky Falkof, Nicky Gyopari, Robin Pridy (editorial support);
Christine Engert, Suzie Johanson, Richard Lloyd, Richard Peters, Alistair Plumb, Jane Prior, Barbara Theisen, Ginny Zeal, Barbara Zuñiga (design support).

Send your thoughts to
books@thomascook.com

- **Found a beach bar, peaceful stretch of sand or must-see sight that we don't feature?**
- **Like to tip us off about any information that needs a little updating?**
- **Want to tell us what you love about this handy, little guidebook and more importantly how we can make it even handier?**

Then here's your chance to tell all! Send us ideas, discoveries and recommendations today and then look out for your valuable input in the next edition of this title. And, as an extra 'thank you' from Thomas Cook Publishing, you'll be automatically entered into our exciting monthly prize draw.

Send an email to the above address or write to:
HotSpots Project Editor, Thomas Cook Publishing, PO Box 227, Unit 15/16, Coningsby Road, Peterborough PE3 8SB, UK.